The Citizen's Guide
to Fighting Government

The Citizen's Guide to
Fighting
Government

FOREWORD BY
**Senator Daniel Patrick
Moynihan**

*Senator Steve Symms
& Larry Grupp*

JAMESON BOOKS, INC. ■ OTTAWA, ILLINOIS

Jameson Books are available at special discounts for bulk purchases for sales promotions, premiums, fund raising or educational use. Special condensed or excerpted editions can also be created to customer specification.

For information and catalog requests write:

Jameson Books, Inc.
P.O. Box 738
Ottawa, IL 61350

Printed in the United States of America.

Distributed to the book trade by Login Brothers Consortium, 1436 West Randolph, Chicago, IL 60607

ISBN: 0–915463–63–6

5   4   3   2   1 / 97   96   95   94

Contents

Foreword

Fighting government is how the United States came about. The government, that is, of George III and the British Parliament, which was seeking to levy taxes from the colonies. These taxes were seen to be necessary because of the huge national debt incurred by Britain in the course of the Seven Years War with France, which we called the French and Indian War. (Few, I suppose, any longer read *The Last of the Mohicans,* but may have seen the recent movie.) Not without reason, many British thought this war was fought not least to protect the colonies from the depredations of Louis XVI of France, and that it was not unreasonable to expect those Bostonians and New Yorkers (where most of the fighting took place) and Virginians (in which conflict George Washington learned soldiering) to pony up a share of the costs. The colonists saw it otherwise. Down at the Battery in New York City, for example, they pulled down an equestrian statue of George III and melted it down for bullets. Soon the British were fighting us. The decisive battle of the Revolutionary War took place at Saratoga on the banks of the Hudson River in upstate New York, a few miles from Lake George where Leatherstocking and the British regulars took such a licking from Montcalm. Word of Burgoyne's surrender was rushed to Versailles. Louis XVI immediately brought France into the war on the side of the colonies, thus incurring a huge debt. This forced him to convene the French equivalent of parliament—the so-called Estates General—to ask them to raise taxes. It was a considerable mistake. Louis lost his head. In the meantime George had lost his colonies.

This is both a cautionary tale for heads of state who would raise taxes, and a perspective I would offer for the consideration of readers of this bold, irreverent, nay, revolutionary text, *The Citizen's Guide to Fighting Government*. Howsoever hallowed the American tradition of restraining the powers of government, Steve Symms and Larry Grupp felt compelled to write a book on fighting contemporary government. This government, which is to say late twentieth century American government, is increasingly characterized by the use of regulation as an instrument of social policy. There are a number of reasons for this. One of these, at least in my view, is that after a half century of war and cold war all around the world, the United States government finds itself hopelessly in debt. This means, among other things, that neither the Executive nor the Congress has a lot of money to spend. Any money to spend! How then to keep busy? Why, of course, by forcing others to spend money in order to comply with regulations promulgated in pursuance of statutes enacted by said Executive and Congress. Regulation has changed the nature of American government. In evidence, let me cite a recent editorial in *Science*, the journal of the American Association for the Advancement of Science, the largest membership organization of its kind in the world. In the interests of full disclosure, as we say in the Senate, let me state that I have served as a vice president and later a member of the board of the AAAS, and have recently been elected a fellow of the association. No matter, *Science* is the best journal of its kind published in the United States. It is just that. A science journal. It has no politics and doesn't need any. But it does from time to time comment on issues where there is an intersection of science and government. Here, then, is the opening paragraph of the editorial of 8 January 1993, written by Philip H. Abelson, deputy editor for engineering and applied sciences.

> On 20 January, the Democrats become sole heirs to a phenomenon of regulation gone amok. In April 1992, fifty-nine regulatory agencies with about 125,000 employees were at work on 4,186 pending regulations. The cost during 1991 of mandates already in place has been estimated at $542 billion. The fastest growing component of costs is environmental regulations, which amounted to $115 billion in 1991 but are slated to grow by more than 50 percent in constant dollars by the year 2000. Twenty years ago, costs of federal environmental regulations were not

visible to the public. However, the number and stringency of unfunded federal requirements have since increased markedly. New and tighter regulations have drained funds from cities, towns, school districts, and individuals. A result is the beginning of a revolt. There is a growing questioning of the factual basis for federal command and control actions and of the scientific competence of the regulators.

An emerging classic example of overreaction is the Superfund legislation that we—the Congress, that is, myself included—rushed into statute in 1980 following the revelations of toxic waste dumping at the Love Canal site in Niagara Falls, New York. We commenced spending some $2 billion a year to clean up "toxic waste sites." A dozen years and billions of dollars later we are beginning to realize, as President Bill Clinton has remarked, that "almost half of all federal Superfund appropriations go to pay lawyers' fees— while 22,000 Superfund sites threaten the health of citizens and communities across America." The problem, very simply, is that government is not good at making science decisions. By and large, there is no such thing as proof in science. Only probability. Scientists live with this without visible strain, but it is too much for a bureaucrat, or at least many such. They want certainty. They don't like to be told that there is no certainty. They do not want citizens to be exposed to risk. They don't like being told that there is no such thing as a risk-free environment of any kind. The real question being, how much risk? And so we get into these painful and expensive binds.

Symms and Grupp—again, in the interest of full disclosure, I must state that Steve Symms and I were the closest of colleagues in the Senate, albeit we hardly agreed on anything—suggest a way out of this bind. More. They show a way out. This book is more than a manifesto. It is a manual for informed citizen participation in government decision making and administration. It is a down-to-earth manual on how to do it yourself. The extraordinary response to Ross Perot's appeal for help to organize a presidential campaign in the spring of 1992, and the continued response to his current organizing effort are testimony to the remarkable potential of volunteer organizations in American public affairs. Symms and Grupp are well to the right of center in most of their politics, but what they are about is at the heart of American government. Their political perspective is one thing; their lessons are universal, including some lessons liberals might usefully learn if we wish to hold our own with these wild frontiersmen!

—Sen. Daniel Patrick Moynihan
Washington, D.C.

Preface

The 1960s and early 1970s were tumultuous. Citizens, and especially students, demonstrated in the streets, rioted, pushed outrageous political agendas, took over public buildings, took college deans hostage, and even bombed a building or two. Yet, by and large, bureaucrats showed little concern at these events. They didn't feel threatened. Why?

Several explanations are possible. For one, the influence of agencies and bureaus was not as pervasive then as it is today. The growth and impact of bureaucratic government since those days has been fantastic. For another, the protesters were, by and large, perceived to be reckless youngsters whom they could dismiss with a shrug.

Now, however, a much different phenomenon is sweeping the land, in the face of a bureaucracy swollen and grown oppressive. Older—traditionally more reserved—citizens are starting to protest virtually criminal abuse on the part of rent control boards, school boards, highway departments, planning and zoning commissions, USFS, OSHA, EPA, FDA, DEA and thousands more similar governmental bodies and self-appointed spokespersons for every cause and every program. Indeed, many citizens have become so incensed at the high-handed usurpation of their freedoms that they are willing to give up their time and risk their savings to fight the bureaucracy. By comparison the kids of the 1960s had little to lose. Protesters today are the entrenched citizens, risking much in their commitment to put things right. Even today's inner-city riots are an expression of the American black's belief that government does not represent his needs, or respond to anything but force.

Only people who perceive that their backs are against the wall go to these lengths. When it involves large numbers of citizens in their later years, real trouble may be brewing. When Mr. and Mrs. Middle America are ready to risk all, they do indeed have the brains, organizational capacity and experience to fight with!

This claim is easily tested by looking closely at those who are in the tax protest and home school movements currently making the headlines. Nearly all are established, otherwise comfortable family people who, in normal circumstances, would never risk their whole world challenging authorities as they do now. That they do is a sure sign how threatened they feel.

An eighty-seven-year-old founding president of a huge corporation recently decided he had had enough. The city in which he made his home imposed foolishly stringent rent controls, among other interventionist ordinances. The net impact was to stop any growth in population, create artificial barriers to construction, and establish a whole new group of homeless indigents, driving out merchants and mummifying the regional economy.

This man could have easily continued his comfortable life as president of the board of a large corporation. But he elected to put his convictions on the line and formed a local Political Action Group. He donated his own money, asked his friends to contribute, hired a director and a spokesman, polled the community, launched a direct mail campaign and bustled to fight the bureaucrats. His friends were astonished. It was the first time they'd even seen him show an interest in active politics.

He ended up changing the law, the city council membership, the planning commission and the mayor, as well as seeing construction of a major complex of three-bedroom apartments in the community. The results, to some, may not seem worth the effort. But this man knew that the community he loved was doomed on its present course. That was all he needed to know. He committed himself.

If there is a message to this book and to the urgency of its advice, it is that the bureaucrats had best contemplate what lies ahead. Lions born in captivity know nothing of freedom. Senior Americans have lived in freedom. They still know what it means, they are smart, and they are acting. These are the activists of the 1990s.

They see the snarled bureaucratic food and drug laws, asbestos laws, environmental regulations that put owls and minnows and bugs and swamps ahead of humans, and a thousand other kinds of red tape. They're sick and tired of bureaucrats and environmental radicals in their twenties dictating whether they may be in business or how they may use their own land.

So far seniors' activities have been limited. Yet the results out in the field have been outstanding whenever they have elected to work in an integrated, well-considered plan. Our gut feeling is that things will change quickly as more citizens come to find that we can follow these leads and change the system.

Introduction

I t may seem that "We the People" have lost the war. Those of us who are concerned about the frightening erosion of our freedoms have lost many battles. No matter what we do, the power and the tyranny of the government grow, unchecked. We get discouraged. But we have not lost all. There is much we can do, and the place to start is with the maxim "know thine enemy."

The proponents of big government and big business have been incredibly effective in promoting their agenda. And that agenda invariably has the effect of taking away our personal freedoms and harming our ability to make a living and care for our families in a manner we deem proper. They keep getting away with it in spite of the candidates we elect and the protests we make—because they study and understand the inner workings of the bureaucratic process much better than we do. But that is something we too can learn and use to put things right.

We who pay the cost for both business and government, who mind our own business, meet our responsibilities, and ask only to be free to live our lives and raise our families, are too often caught napping. We expect others to be as decent and responsible as ourselves but some are not. These people care nothing about right and wrong. They are out to win, and they do. When they do, all we do is complain instead of fighting back. "Our" writers and experts analyze the damage, name the culprits, warn us of new catastrophes in the works—but give us no road map or plan to get out of the swamp.

A political analyst, evaluating the recent national elections, found that only 53 percent of the eligible voters went to the polls.

This is not because of apathy, as the media would have us believe, but because we perceive that our government is no longer ours— that is, responsive to us and controlled by men and women account- able to us at election time. In a sense we are not governed at all any more, but rather *ruled*. Our rulers are arrogant, always power-hun- gry, faceless bureaucrats, who somehow believe they don't have to answer to anyone, even to God. Many citizens conclude from this that voting doesn't settle very much. They are correct, at least for now. The time is past when we can think we have done our duty by going to the polls.

However, many of the junior dictators adversely affecting our lives are those from our own community. They serve on rent con- trol boards, school boards, planning and zoning commissions and other agencies over which we are supposed to have direct control. Even if we have lost some of that control, there are techniques avail- able to reassert ourselves and call them to task. We have to learn how, and that's what this book is about. Then we have to do it. And by taking back our communities, we send a message to Washing- ton, D.C., that its time of running roughshod over our lives is ending.

The day-to-day working rules for imposing accountability on bureaucrats, politicians, the media, boards and councils, etc., are not insurmountably complex. To be sure, applying these rules and creating an effective force to restore freedom can tax the ability of even our smarter, better-organized people. Yet the authors' experi- ence indicates that we can learn these techniques, and that we do have many intelligent, well organized people on our side. In our view, once this group hears the bugle and decides to march, it can accomplish everything it sets out to do.

Some of the techniques we must use are closely held industry secrets. The direct mail industry, for instance, will take great issue with our reducing its business down to twenty-one logical rules. The media will never, under any circumstances, admit that they could be manipulated as we, the authors, suggest they might in the following chapters.

This book will not recite a litany of government abuses. If the reader does not already believe we have a serious problem, this is not the text of choice. But those who know the way things are and are ready to fight back will find a detailed, succinct road map in these pages.

For some, including both authors, the process has become an end in itself. A lifetime in this business would not have been possible if it were not enjoyable. Yet it is painfully obvious that more of us will have to start working smarter rather than harder, or we will certainly lose the few freedoms remaining. We welcome any additions to these ranks of freedom fighters, and wish you all well.

We would like to add that our rallying call is not exclusive, sectarian or limited to any political stripe. We genuinely wish to help all Americans who want to take the government into their own hands. We do not believe that any constituency, be it liberal or conservative, populist or single-issue, wants the government to operate as it does now to limit our individual freedom.

Fighting Government is a how-to book, a shop manual, not a theoretical tract. Citizens should discuss fixing what has gone wrong in our political process, but that is not our concern here. This is a book about *using* the existing system, to recapture our lives and work, rather than reforming it.

It is the authors' honest intent to empower people to get the government out of their lives. With a bit of luck and a good effort by dedicated freedom fighters, the government may again become one "of the people, by the people, and for the people," and not a power unto itself.

Chapter 1

Forming a Political Action Group

"Hello. This is Gene Epply," the caller explained somewhat excitedly. "Your friend, Mr. Tollhous in Seattle, gave me your name.

"I have a subdivision project started near Seattle. Some opponents have organized a protest group and gone to the city asking that the project be stopped on phony environmental grounds. I understand you can help me organize a group that can become a political counterweight to the one opposing me. Is it possible that you can come over in the next day or so and explain how I can get organized?"

The caller already knew he had to form a Political Action Group.

Political problems involving battle with the bureaucracy are most effectively undertaken under the umbrella of a larger citizen organization. Those who think big government solves people's problems—we'll call them the Other Side—are adept at forming groups and more groups, typically in order to pass more laws or to force bureaucrats to act on behalf of their freedom-stealing agendas. They organize even to pursue what seem like minor issues. Freedom lovers may not like doing things like this. They often find it unprincipled or bad manners or busybody or grubby or "one of those things that good people don't do." And that is why they keep getting drubbed by an enemy who has no such scruples. Freedom is constantly under attack in this politicized age. Therefore all who love freedom *must* face a hard fact: *they too must organize in order to defend themselves.* There is seldom any good alternative when your rights and property are threatened by the Other Side. Like our founding fathers, we must "associate together" for the common goal.

The Bigger, the Better

The new group will do best if it is fairly large (which is not to rule out smaller ones). Large groups make things easier because the greater numbers command more attention from the media and will be impossible for politicians to ignore.

Elected officials tend to be responsive because they simply cannot ignore a large bloc of potential voters. Media people will be fearful that a large Political Action Group may represent the next area of public interest. Ignoring it may cause the newsroom to miss the next groundswell. Chances are that 90 percent of the media won't like what you are doing—since today's reporters and editors are lopsidedly dedicated to the proposition that enough government can fix anything—but they won't ignore the issue if the group is sizable, or merely appears large.

Thus, most effective groups appear to have large numbers, or claim to represent many people. This is so even though, in fact, they are usually controlled by a small, focused, internal group that guides the parent group toward its ends. Unless your group gets big very quickly it is prudent to be just a touch vague about your membership figures and give them a rosy interpretation. But the number must in all cases be credible, or chances are slim that the group will be successful.

Small groups of dedicated believers can do much, so don't be discouraged if you don't get a large membership right away. A small team can be disruptive, colorful and highly visible. Even a handful of focused people can call attention to their goals and may in time achieve them. Some groups learn crowd-gathering techniques and grow like mushrooms. Others are coldly calculated from their inception to remain small. Some may be ad hoc, temporary affairs to take advantage of a timely issue. *The important thing is always that some effort be made and that somebody be there to take charge.* When people are incensed they will act—if there is a leader to point the way.

Big-Name Power

Prestige associates can give your group clout, just as big member-ship can. Groups can profit immensely by being identified with big names and powers-that-be in the community, especially in the early days of organizing. Three approaches are common:

1. Recruiting a big-name board of directors. They bring credibil-ity, instant recognition to the cause, and the capacity to raise some fairly easy money.

    The downside to using "name" people is that they are too busy and self-protecting to get involved with a half-hearted or poorly-planned effort that they feel has little chance of suc-cess. You'll have to be on your toes every minute. Also, "names" as a rule will not do any of the real work. They may insist that everything be done by professional staff and overseen by an administrative board. Many groups find this is a luxury they can't afford.
2. The star system. Should the issue be risky and uncertain in out-come, the organizers may find they can recruit but one or two "heavy hitters." This may still seem attractive, but we do not recommend it. Two "stars" are not enough to be effective and often do not work well with the rank and file.

    Try appointing these people as honorary cochairmen, know-ing the actual committee work must be done by an adminis-trative board. They will not come to your meetings, participate in the activities, nor have much of a voice in making policy or plans. The risk in this is that the media may corner them and ask about issues or how the group is handling it. The "stars" may start talking and never stop till they have done irrepara-ble harm. Therefore, honorary officers must take interest in the group and be briefed regularly by someone actively involved.
3. A professional spokesman. No one affects the group's success more than its spokesman, so finding a pro is a big plus. Some of these people have the gift to stand right up and speak force-fully on almost any subject.

    The often insurmountable problem for the freedom fighter is finding this type of person to lead the campaign. They do exist but there aren't many. Nevertheless, there may be a Meryl Streep or a Charlton Heston who genuinely believes in your cause. Take a chance. Call somebody.

All three approaches are limited by access to "names" and the inherent problems of working with giant egos. Your PAG may do well simply to use a core group of unfamous but genuinely interested and dedicated citizens. This can also be a plus with the media, who often sympathize with everyday folk trying to make a difference.

Naming Your PAG

Get the maximum impact from the group's name. Bring your best people in to brainstorm the name and aim for the most descriptive, strident, easy-to-remember name your group can live and work with.

Use as many buzz words in the group name as possible. The acronym should make a social statement as well as be easy to remember—for instance, NOW and ACT-UP. The old Another Mother for Peace showed that a name doesn't have to be short to be catchy. Make a list of words that fit your cause and brainstorm them to see what short, fitting acronyms you can make of them. Time spent studying potential names is instructive and can even help focus your group purpose.

Timing

Issues come and go. Your group effort has to be timed and tuned correctly or it is wasted. The plan of action may work flawlessly in one moment and fall flat a month later. You have to focus your action on a concept ("stop this construction!" "we need tax relief!") that fits the public mood *now*. The Other Side folk are masters at seizing opportunities that few of us realize exist. Our Side must learn to sail when the wind blows.

Accurate timing is not too difficult. Experienced groups use the following tests:

1. Is the issue in the media? Are people talking about the concept you'll focus on?

2. Are people waiting in the wings for a leader or for a group that will support the concept?

Remember, it doesn't necessarily take lots of people to be effective; if the "dedicated" few would rather stay home and watch TV just now, your timing is wrong!

3. Do you see potential supporters among the opinion setters in the community you want to influence?
4. Under the worst circumstances, can enough of the faithful be assembled to give at least the illusion of credibility?

Most of us, especially community and business leaders and anybody with a full-time job, tend to be reluctant to do the necessary grunt work in the precincts. The willingness of ordinary people to do this work is an indication that the issue is timely.

5. Can money be raised to support the group's stand on the issue?

Raising money is truly the key issue when evaluating timing. The most reliable way to poll your chances of success is a fund appeal. Efforts to collect money and recruit influential people are a quick study for evaluating timeliness and are amazing in their ability to winnow wheat from tares.

Obstacles Ahead

Working people start at a big disadvantage when attempting to regain or expand their freedom in the political arena. Like it or not, we must admit that freedom has no direct constituency. It doesn't pay anything to insist on what's right. You can't take the freedom you seek to the bank. Yet when we see quiet, ordinary citizens with nothing to gain coming forward, we can be pretty sure that something is seriously amiss in the system and that it has to be corrected or reformed.

We can be just as sure that reform will be fiercely resisted. Bureaucratic high-handedness has a potent, built-in constituency. Freedom issues slash bureaucratic budgets, reduce spheres of influence, decrease the need for regulators and generally decrease the number of government employees (a powerful voting bloc with time on their hands for organizing). These are direct assaults on the self-interest of bureaucrats, politicians and all their camp followers who suck up our tax dollars. You know they will organize and fight tooth and nail to retain their power.

Our Side has trouble recruiting because there are no jobs, power, money, authority, or bread and games to offer those who help us, even when we are wildly successful. We do what we do primarily because it is right, and good for us. But beware of a trap in this! We can't afford to be holier-than-thou about it. When out looking for help, Middle America is too often its own worst enemy. With distressing frequency freedom's advocates drive potential helpers away because the latter seem to us to lack political, social or religious purity. We think, "We can't allow this group to join us because it's in the wrong party, it has a money interest in this issue, it's not clean."

This thinking is a big mistake. For example, anti-abortion groups are often neutralized internally because the Roman Catholics do not want to associate with evangelical fundamentalists. Union members have not been accepted by factory owners who could have benefited by their support for more open zoning regulations. What good can we do if the group doesn't function? None.

The rule is simply this. We're in this to expand or regain our freedom and we do nothing if we don't win. The organizing group should always keep that uppermost. It should define its mission narrowly, accept whatever support is forthcoming, and shoot to win. Politics can—and in fact should—make some strange bedfellows. This does not mean that the various mismatched groups will end up accepting each other's total program or values; only that, in this one situation, we all smell the skunk so we join together to get rid of it.

The "who" question is not so important. Some improbable and ragtag armies won amazing victories over the bureaucracy in the 1970s and 1980s. The important things are seeing the common enemy and recognizing that we must organize together to defend ourselves and our freedom. With those understandings freedom fighters are ready to act. This book is written to tell them how to win.

Chapter 2

Setting Goals

I t's tough to organize without a goal. If you haven't set a firm goal before initial organization, the very next step is to work out your aims for the group and write a brief statement of purpose that all can agree to. Articulated goals for the group should be very simple. Everyone who hears of the group should be clear about its mission.

Do not confuse your goal with a strategy and blueprint for action—the means you will use to attain it. You should be able to write down your goal in one sentence (even if you choose to expand it a bit in your statement of purpose). In contrast, action plans developed by the group's strategists will probably be complex and certainly will not be publicly disclosed. Goal setting is simply identifying what the group wants done, and in a way that you want both your members and the public to know. The goal should not be so limited or narrow as to name whose budget you wish to chop, which bureaucrat you want transferred, the departments you want dissolved, who should be fired or unelected, which law should be changed, etc. These are tactical matters.

Examples of goals we want: unrestricted home schools; land for a dump; approval of a new medication; land withdrawn from a wilderness area; the right to build a home on property along a creek; and so on.

And just as important: After you formulate and announce the group's goal in simple, agreed terms, *stick to it*. Never deviate from that goal. It is the focus of all your group activity and without it you are adrift. Obviously, then, you have to set the right goal at the outset. This will not always be easy. Different members will have varying ideas about what the group exists for. Many times it is tough to reach agreement on exactly what it is that everyone wants done. You can overcome opposition in many cases with broader wording (though keeping your target in the gun sights). Make your statement of purpose so inclusive that everyone can go along with it.

Another rule is, "Never debate the pros and cons of the group's political position within the support group." When setting goals, speaking for the cause to the faithful, be cautious that absolute purity of purpose is always maintained. Leadership should never acknowledge that the opposition may have a point. In this regard there is little place in a Political Action Group for internal philosophical debate. Wannabe philosophers should be encouraged to practice their rhetoric in more informal settings among friends who are also recreational debaters.

Union members know this rule well. Management is always, always the bad guy. The group is always opposed to and suspicious of management's motives. No "trying to understand the other guy's point of view" is ever tolerated.

When you have picked the target, it must then be personalized and frozen. This polarizes the debate and lays exclusive claim to one's followers. Often, but not always, the goal is frozen in the title chosen for the Political Action Group. For instance, CAPZ—Citizens Against Planning and Zoning—says it all. "Freezing" is most often done when developing the strategy, but can sometimes occur when setting the original goals of the group.

Having set the goal and agreed not to be deterred from it, publicize the fact. Loud and clear. Let the group of supporters who are represented by the effort know where they are going and that their individual efforts will be needed to take them there. Be diligent about announcing the existence of the group and its objective, but never, never, never divulge the group's strategy, except to the closest supporters and in strictest confidence.

All that the larger group should know (and you should make certain that members do know) is that the strategy exists.

Widely acclaimed public notice puts everyone supporting the effort on notice that sympathizers will have to perform. The certain existence of a well developed strategy gives the rank and file hope that the effort is organized and will eventually be successful.

To summarize:

1. Set simple, easy-to-understand goals for the group.
2. Polarize the issue. Never publicly recognize the middle ground.
3. Be cautious that the opposition is never able to switch your group away from its original announced goal, while you are always alert to the possibility of diverting your opponents.
4. Announce the goal to the membership and the world. Put everyone on record.
5. Personalize the target. We are going after specific members of the bureaucracy.
6. Develop a well-thought-through political strategy that will accomplish the goal (as outlined in future chapters).

Chapter 3

Brain Trust

From 1976 to 1980 Ronald Reagan, when he was running for president, used only one speech outline. He varied the opening and closing a bit to suit specific audiences, but other than the opening containing a few local issues and names, the presentation remained much the same. Reagan polled often so as to be able to detect changes in the country's mood. He was a skilled speaker and could have changed his speech, but found it was better if he stuck to the basics. Some small adjustments would be made as necessary but generally he talked about the perceived important current issues—the ones people were concerned about and would identify with, in terms that made sense to them.

Polling gave Reagan this information but a brain trust will do just as well on the local level. A brain trust is an old political device, going back to days before polling, to tap opinion in the community. A politician would get together a committee of savvy local leaders to assess the public mood and plan appropriate political strategies. This kind of brain trust is still extremely useful to a Political Action Group. It is—the brains. It handles political intelligence. Setting up the brain trust is perhaps the next logical step, or at least a very early step. It will be needed to set strategy and put the issues into the right words.

In the days before polling, an aspiring mayor, councilman or sheriff would call together six or eight of the wisest, most "street smart" residents he could find, and ask them to meet with him twice a week for breakfast to answer just three questions. Limiting the discussion by your brain trust to a few subjects is important—since smart people have opinions on everything—but focusing on what is important to the candidate is important, so discipline is necessary.

Political campaigns quickly settle down to addressing four or five major issues, and a good brain trust will not only provide early and solid advice on these issues, but also serve as an inexpensive substitute for polling if funds are not available for that.

The questions for a PAG brain trust are not so different from what they have always been: What are the issues of concern to the community or region? What is the feeling among the constituents about these problems? What does John Q. Public want done about these problems? How and in what words should we address these issues to the probable satisfaction of the public?

Knowing the issues and having answers gives the group spokesman an opportunity to rehearse his speech before appearing before voters. This is also painfully important when dealing with mean, obstreperous bureaucrats, especially if we must take our case to the general public.

The device may initially be perceived to be hopelessly populist in nature, sometimes to the extent that freedom fighters may eschew its use. It is an example of issues being important in terms of how they are articulated rather than what they actually are; of phrasing over substance. But couching the issue in language that is palatable to the average citizen only seems to make good sense.

If your budget doesn't allow for polling (covered later in this book) a brain trust can predict trends effectively at a local level. Knowing how to address the issues satisfactorily is vital to political victory. Contests with bureaucrats can be won by people who know how to place the issues in the proper perspective for the citizen and the media. The battle is for the hearts and minds of potential supporters. Our Side must make better use of the PR opportunities extended to us.

During these modern times, when polling is a mature and well defined technology, the principal function of the brain trust is to help develop a winning strategic plan and to advise the campaign on a continuing basis. The strategy may be written by the committee, by one or two key members, or by a paid professional who will stay in very close touch with the brain trust during the writing phase. Their input will continually be sought. In addition to this strategy there are hundreds of small, tactical issues ranging from "how do we change laws" to "what do we include in the group slide show" that must be addressed.

It is also the duty of the brain trust to come up with good, valid, day-to-day ideas that will get the group from the point of stating its goal to ultimate success. Political operatives will find that this may include dozens of aspects of the campaign ranging from suggested news conference ideas to raising money.

Tough, street smart, yet politically sensitive people are needed for this sort of job. The champions of regulation have had an advantage in volunteer numbers since the Great Depression of the 1930s or earlier. In addition they could promise to key volunteers, or to their group, lucrative jobs in the bloated bureaucracy they created, as a reward for good service.

The Other Side's advantage is dwindling. Big government looks worse every day as more of us are forced to fight for our basic rights. As more and more people learn the techniques to restore lost freedom, our work will stop being nearly impossible and become merely difficult.

Chapter 4

Board of Directors

M ost effective groups of any kind or purpose in our society function best with some sort of governing body at the helm. Someone or a group of someones must have responsibility for the success or failure of the group's endeavor. Putting a board of directors in place first can lead to a point of conflict with organizers who see other priorities as more important. The authors' experience leads them to believe that the brain trust is the first, most important management team to put in place. At times it isn't even vitally important that a full, true board of directors be organized. A group chairman or spokesman may do nicely.

The rule of thumb when deciding if the group would benefit by even worrying about a board of directors is to go ahead and organize a board—after the brain trust is properly staffed and if there are still qualified business-oriented people left over to handle the chores of board members. Surrounding the political action goals of the group with as many smart people as possible is never inappropriate.

Call it a board of directors, a steering committee, or the management group, its traditional function for any Political Action Group is pretty much the same. It is the business or management arm of the group. The board (or whatever it is called) must be relatively small, made up of people who have a wide range of talents and are used to arriving at good, valid decisions via consensus. The single, most important fact that every board must face is that it must make decisions.

Boards should not try to be the brain trust. A good board will understand that this is not its function. The brain trust is only one element of the campaign. The media expert, research analyst, spokesman, fund raiser, newsletter editor, bookkeeper, etc., are all important, but perhaps not equal elements of the campaign.

Boards should oversee all of these but, in most cases, should not become involved with the day-to-day management and operation of these functions. Boards that involve themselves in minutiae will rapidly degenerate into impotence. The only exception might include the operations of fund raising. Keeping extremely close track of fund raising efforts and the cash stream these produce seems to be incredibly important. Boards that closely monitor the major money can usually be characterized as being in control and knowledgeable.

In that regard, boards should meet frequently. No less than two to three hours once a week during a hot campaign, or whatever time it takes to efficiently get the work done. The paid staff should prepare a detailed list of major bills for approval along with a current budget reflecting the impact of these and prior bills. Income—actual and projected—must also be itemized for the board's perusal.

All board meetings should operate with a printed agenda. Doing otherwise invites longer, potentially divisive meetings which risk alienating some board members. Board agendas should be closed twelve hours before the board meets. Any board member or major staffer should have the option of adding agenda items—before closing—by contacting the chairman.

It is best to discourage group members from coming to the board meetings other than as observers. Petty comments and complaints often take too much of the board's valuable time. Instead, let members talk to board members informally when they have observations or comments.

The board chair is sometimes the spokesman for the group (whose role is discussed in another chapter). Election of the chairman-spokesman is usually done shortly after the board first organizes. The board may, as appropriate, recruit a volunteer spokesman other than the chairman, or hire a person with these talents.

All major staff people should be required to report regularly regarding the function of the element of the campaign over which they have responsibility. Coordinators having responsibility for major portions of the campaign such as research, speakers bureau, literature distribution, legal or whatever, who are also volunteers, must be asked to report even more frequently than paid staffers. Their situation must be viewed with a bit more charity, both because they are volunteers and because they are usually new to the job. It takes a board chairman with a great deal of tact and skill to draw out, support and handle volunteers correctly.

One of the most pressing initial orders of business for the board after election of officers and chairman is to develop a mechanism whereby minutes are kept and tenure is established. A certain amount of dedication is built into the group by the members knowing exactly how long they will serve. Knowing that abilities and strengths will rotate with the board members also seems to give the membership additional confidence in their board. Often this little structural device is overlooked. Traditionally, effective board members possess four *W*'s (Wealth, Wisdom, Work and Willingness).

Keeping good, valid minutes is extremely important for helping the board proceed without wobbling toward its objective. Minutes should always crisply and succinctly reflect what was done. Only rarely should they detail what was said.

We have often been told that a group is too small to justify a board. "Our effort is tiny and fleeting," they say in so many words, "it has no need to be so formal." Not so; it always pays handsomely to organize. Someone has to be in ultimate control and call the shots.

Waning interest and resulting non-attendance on the part of board members are sometimes a problem. Our experience has been that if a board is genuinely in control of a project, reviewing its progress, approving the bills, supervising its income and operating professionally with printed minutes, a schedule of accounts, a printed agenda, etc., interest during a spirited campaign will not suffer. Board members of the quality required to win will be interested in managing events even if their immediate commitment to the cause occasionally flags.

Probably the greater real-life danger than waning interest is the possibility that the board will start micromanaging the project. Occasionally the board may have to step in when one of the elements of the campaign is obviously not being handled in a timely, expeditious manner. However, if—as is all too common—the board begins to make little, day-to-day decisions normally handled by the staff, it is a sure sign that the board is composed of amateurs who have little idea how boards function best. That is one more reason to choose the board from the most successful persons in the business community: they know how organization works.

Fund raisers, professional office staff, professional organizers, brain trust chairmen should all make their own day-to-day operating decisions, subject to policy and budgets set by the board. Budgets always reflect the operational philosophy of the group. Where the board decides to put its money reflects what is very important and what is considered to be less important. Staffers should not be concerned about their place in the campaign structure, except for knowing what resources are available to them.

Group Spokesman

An effective group spokesman is almost essential to success. The position should be filled with care, as early as possible. He or she will be continually visible as the representative and symbol of the group to the media, the opposition, the public, and (of great importance) to the group's own members. The spokesman must be presentable, dedicated, knowledgeable and articulate.

Who the spokesman should *not* be is important too. This position should not be confused with the campaign manager, fund raiser, media director or any of the other specialized positions that may be part of a successful political action. Organizing and directing a political effort are a full-time job in and of themselves. To ask one person to assume both manager and spokesman roles is needlessly asking for trouble, unless the effort is small.

Spokesmen should be able to think well on their feet and handle pressure situations. Look for someone who's intelligent, outgoing, gregarious and—most of all—blessed with a sense of humor. A friendly laugh can defuse a confrontational situation or win an audience or poke mischievous fun at the Other Side's views.

A knack for salesmanship is a huge plus in your spokesman. In fact, much of the job is a kind of selling. Certainly fund raising is a salesman's art. He or she must also "sell" the group's goal, its sincerity, its desire to carry through with the project, its understanding of the issues, its need for more members, and so on.

The group's talker will probably appear on local radio and TV talk shows, in the group video, perhaps in its slide show and—if the group does them—in TV commercials. Nothing helps more in these situations than what is called *presence* in the business. Presence is loosely defined as the ability to dominate a situation by simply being there physically. In our experience it's something you have or don't have, not something anyone can learn. Tutoring might add a little veneer with a lot of effort but it's not worth it. Look for someone who has presence to begin with!

A strong philosophical commitment to the PAG's agenda is a strong plus but certainly not an absolute requirement. Our opponents, for instance, are very good about bringing in celebrity-type people who are trained public speakers for use by their groups, knowing that these people are not 100 percent consistent on all the issues but that they are committed on this one. At the same time, avoid a spokesman with known or strongly suspected antipathy to the PAG's view, or those with a hired-gun image.

Some celebrity talents like to blow into town to hype a project, but are reluctant to stay with it to its conclusion. There is nothing wrong with using a dose of hype in a campaign so long as the steering committee realizes that it is not a substitute for a group spokesman. On the other hand, using relatively famous, respected local people with natural speaking ability is fine, so long as these people are willing to commit full time to the project to see it through to its conclusion.

The rule always is to try to select a spokesman with as broad an appeal as possible. A good place to start looking is among attorneys, preachers, teachers and businesses. These groups are used to speaking and being before the public. If they themselves can't help, they may steer you to someone who can. The authors have often found a good spokesman through such recommendations. As long as the individual has a strong commitment to winning, we try to minimize the fact that he may not be 100 percent rock solid sound on our complete range of issues. Also, avoid people who are recognized, habitual spokesmen. Their effect and your money and effort are diluted by their overexposure.

At times groups have been so desperate for an adequate spokesman that they have considered hiring one. Unfortunately, good professional spokesmen are seldom available. Nevertheless, a paid position makes some sense because of the huge amount of time one must dedicate to the project. Often twenty hours per week is the minimum, and a burden up to sixty hours is common. A professional spokesman is worth considering if you can find one.

One last area to take into account is the range of duties your spokesman will have. Here are a few guidelines. When the group is just getting launched, the spokesman may set up a speakers bureau, work on the slide show, and otherwise prepare presentations he will later use in public. However, as the press of daily duties takes over, he can no longer be tied down to these functions. Some spokesmen we've known have chaired the steering committee/board of directors. Others have not, choosing instead to meet with these people as one of the body in an ex-officio capacity. Let the spokesman decide; either way works well. The spokesman will necessarily meet often with the brain trust and, to a certain extent, take a day-to-day hand with those raising money. He should coach the office staff and/or volunteers working on the project so that they know how best to handle citizen input. All of this sounds as if the spokesman will be very busy indeed, and often he is just that! But his overall role should be viewed not as the do-it-all type but as the master of ceremonies urging all in the group toward their goal.

Some few political projects do not require a spokesman. However, if there is any element of public relations mixed in the undertaking, the group is handicapped without a good spokesman.

The checklist below takes into consideration the facts that (a) the spokesman is extremely important and (b) he will be difficult to identify and recruit.

1. Spread the word among the group that a spokesman will be essential to the success of the project. Review the duties of the speaker (in detail) with the organizers. Get everyone to start thinking and talking about finding the correct person.
2. Survey the various members of the group who got the project started. Observe their dress, deportment and presence. Dress is the first, most immediately obvious guideline. Credible spokesmen will already be dressing for success.
3. Get out in the community, talking to likely prospects.
4. Look at other groups similar to yours when there are some in the community.
5. Consider the service clubs, chambers of commerce or even

church groups as sources of spokesmen. The Toastmasters are a rich local source for talent.

6. Review rosters of retired business people and legislators who might have both the time and the ability.

7. Start early, make a decision early and then run with it.

If in the end one good spokesman fails to materialize, try using co-spokesmen. That allows the better of the two to emerge under trial by fire. Putting two people in the one job invariably leads to one doing the work, but relieves the one's fear about having an impossible burden.

Finally, there is no way to overemphasize finding your group's representative from day one. No real, effective engagement with the opposition will occur until the spokesman is ready to go.

Chapter 6

The News Conference

O ur opponents seem to be masters at orchestrating their news conferences. The snake oil they can peddle this way is amazing.

Would-be regulators call the media together to show them a crack in the ground, then straight-facedly advise that the crack will grow into a rift running through a power plant, that the power plant is therefore too risky, that we don't need the power anyway, that construction has killed all the trees in the valley, that the trees call the rain and that, as a result, we should learn to live without electrical energy because the region will become a desert anyway.

Holding a news conference is something that our side needs to learn to do much better. It is a bit of an art, but one your group can master.

The first law is always this: Let there be news in every news conference. The media hate being used as sincerely as they love finding something new. Think up a vital reason for the conference. There are many others but these are proven winners:

1. Announcing the formation of the Political Action Group, including the intended objectives. Also valuable as a means of putting the group on public record.
2. Announcing that the Political Action Group has secured uncommonly famous personalities as co-chairmen, chairman, speakers or as legal counsel.
3. Attacking the bureaucracy—pointing out gross injustices we were being asked to suffer while maintaining a refusal to do so in silence.

4. Introducing an "average citizen" to the media and allowing them to quiz that person about his or her encounters with the system—especially horror stories about the bureaucracy we are trying to chastise.
5. Answering charges on the part of the opposition. (Since it is the authors' preference to remain on the offensive, we do not care for this method of operation or reason for a news conference. Opponents should react to our timing and be calling news conferences in response to our charges.)
6. Announcing the successful completion of a significant phase of the project.

If possible, call the media a day ahead to alert them to the event. Either call the media yourself or designate a single secretary who will handle the chore on a continuing basis. Building a relationship with the media is an important skill that should be nurtured by having the same person call time after time. After calling, we often send out a perfunctory reminder card.

A professional press person is best for this work. If one isn't available, or if a salary isn't available, assign the post to a volunteer. A personal, friendly rapport with the individual members of the press is often an essential link in convincing a reporter that you have a story.

Mastering the art of holding news conferences in unique locations, while very tough, is certainly worth the effort in terms of impact. We have gone to jails, penitentiaries, asylums, kitchens, planning and zoning meetings, bank vaults and stockyards, among others, in an attempt to dramatize our point.

News conferences on the courthouse steps are stale. A more dramatic location is tempting to the media, which are always looking for colorful, thirty-second background segments. You might, for instance, pick a stockyard. When reporters ask why, tell them the location is to dramatize the political BS we have to contend with. The device will bring them running unless the organizing group is so old and tired it has absolutely no credibility left.

Since finding these types of locations is very much an art and definitely not learned, our recommendation is to stay alert for opportunities and then boldly seize them.

Here's a checklist of suggestions and requirements for the conference:

1. Hold the conference in a common spot with which everyone in the Fourth Estate and one's supporters are familiar. Since 70 percent of Americans get most of their information from television, make the location a "telegenic" one somehow connected to the topic. If possible, have visible displays.
2. Provide plenty of parking.
3. Obtain a spacious room for TV crews who must be able to get their equipment into the news conference room without undue problems. Walk-up, third-floor offices are obviously a poor choice.
4. Provide plenty of chairs, electrical outlets, a speaker's podium with jacks for sound equipment, and telephones at hand. (Costs are more than trivial and have to be taken into account in advance.)
5. The room should be thoroughly checked out for glitches or problems by the Political Action Group. If need be, call in a professional to do it.
6. The conference must start promptly at the agreed-on time. (But be flexible to major market media.)
7. Consider the various deadlines represented in the media when establishing the time for the news conference.
8. All facts, data and conclusions that will be presented must be carefully researched and logically presented.
9. Arrange time for one-on-one interviews after the conference. Help each reporter find and develop his angle.

No matter where the conference is held, be sure plenty of well-written news releases are available. Attendance will be much better if the media people know much of their work will be done for them including:

1. Interesting news releases.
2. Glossy photos as appropriate.
3. TV video and photo opportunities.
4. Charts and graphs and other visuals that explain the situation.

5. Opportunities to question and interview the organizers and participants in the conference.

What is news varies from day to day. Gauge the relative interest of your news against what is on the wires and on TV. You get a better response for a release on a slow news day. A release or conference that is relevant to current world or national news will give local media their own angle. They may indulge you with big play against a big event.

One way to keep your finger on the news pulse is to subscribe to the Associated Press newswire. The AP news service is available through inexpensive computer network subscriptions. No PAG can afford to be without it. Be sure, too, to get your conference listed on the AP Day Book, a schedule of upcoming events and conferences. Reporters and editors check the Day Book for stories. Local equivalents shouldn't be ignored, either. Provide the local TV, radio and papers with your schedule at the first opportunity.

Many experienced pros try putting out donuts, coffee and sandwiches at news conferences held at 11:00 A.M. The media people will holler that this doesn't make a bit of difference, but after an event or two with free goodies, in the authors' experience, the attendance always seemed about as good as it could ever get.

Conventional wisdom holds that the overall impact of a press conference is maximized by a silver-tongued speaker. Glibness certainly counts heavily but not universally. There are times when an overcoached aw-shucks, obviously nervous, obviously unskilled amateur can make a great impression. If done correctly and with purpose, media people tend to believe such a person. The device is especially effective when there is danger that the media and public feel the group in question is a high-powered, slick organization about to run over ignorant, common people. It's always important to get as many of your own group to the event as possible, and the more so when their presence belies a "slick" image. You want your troops to *be* the common people shown in the TV news spot.

The authors are often asked what to do when the opposition has a news conference. Depending on your own chutzpah quotient, you may choose to send your designated spokesman to your opposition's media circuses. Be sure the spokesman is ready to stage his own "impromptu" news conference on the spot. When this works well, it is great fun, but normally your response is handled better at your own news conference the next day. It gives the opponents the undivided spotlight at their time and gives you yours, later ... which is better.

Supposing you do crash the Other Side's party, send one or two of your most knowledgeable, most articulate speakers to the conference. Instruct them to wear your buttons and your name tags. If you have been doing your own homework, the media people will recognize your people and, as soon as the bad guys are finished, will rush to you for comment. It's risky since your people will have to think well in a clutch, but instead of the Other Side having a solo news conference, you have one as well, however informally.

If you're aware that ineffective spokesmen for the Other Side are in the vicinity, for example at a state fair, holding your press conference nearby and then sending the media over to interview untrained opponents will help your cause immeasurably.

If the opposition catches on to this scheme and tries to stage the same thing, your organization should adopt a system of name tags given out by a secretary at the door. By this time the media people should all be known to the group. Should one show up by surprise, a tag can be made on the spot.

If the opponents try to enter your conference, ask them why they are there. Usually they will ask if the event is open to the public. Tell them yes, to public supporters. It is rare that they will not accept your suggestion to wait outside till it is over.

Screening participants does not work in public places, however, so if you choose such a spot, you'll just have to be ready for enemy questions.

All in all, you can't make your political point until you are heard, so plan on using press conferences as often as you have fresh ways to get the word out.

Chapter 7

Dealing with
the Media

Most experienced people on Our Side would agree that the reason the media usually treat us so badly is that our klutz factor is so extremely high ... and maybe a bit of bias against independent operators. Dealing with the media takes skill, integrity, research and lots and lots of good, old-fashioned, sweat-producing effort—attributes that seem to be in short supply among those who want to get the government off their backs. Whenever you have taken the time to put some effort into the relationship, you will be fairly treated. It's like being married. A really good marriage doesn't just happen.

Political activists who are handling the media should make all the calls regarding news conferences, interviews, press parties, etc., personally. Get to know the people at the various offices. Learn their personal interests, preferences and orientations. When holding a news conference, meet them personally, greeting each by name. This capitalizes on the rule that says it's tough to do a mean, biting story about someone you know personally and respect.

Carry this a step further if one of the media people runs a false, misleading, inaccurate story about your group; call him up and tell him very nicely that you would like to have lunch. A discussion limited to the facts, data and perhaps to some extent their interpretation, can be very constructive.

Keep the professional wants and needs of the media people uppermost:

- They want a by-line.
- They want the story picked up by the national wire or network.
- They all want prizes.
- They all want ego-gratification.
- They all have biases (we all do) that need to be fed.
- They all want exclusives.

Reporters also want to sell their station, paper or channel to the best of their ability. Each has different requirements that will make that happen. Therefore:

1. Provide many visuals for TV. This many include models, charts, prerecorded videos of one-time events.
2. Provide some visuals for the paper including B&W glossies so they can run good, flattering pictures with the story rather than an embarrassing photo of a supporter sitting at his own news conference asleep or some such similar photo.
3. Keep accurate track of each person's needs and production requirements. If necessary, go early to a selected few with the story on the condition that they not break it until the agreed-on time (so that they have time to prep in competition with everyone else). TV, radio and print media are all different.
4. Do not try to tell them how to write the story or ask to pre-screen it before release. This is an amateur faux pas that our groups commit all too frequently.
5. Do not try to fool them or go out with poorly written or researched information. Never prevaricate. Change how the story is explained, but *don't lie.*
6. Be very sensitive to each person's deadline. Keep track of it. Discuss deadlines when calls are made announcing conferences. Keep in mind that TV people will always want to be ready with something for both their 6:00 P.M. news and the 10:00 P.M. edition.
7. Keep track of who is working for whom. This changes dramatically and with frightening frequency. The master media list should be updated with names and deadlines every time a contact is made.
8. Most major cities now have but one major newspaper. Find out if it is an evening or morning paper and accommodate its sched-

ule. Giving the radio people (who have very little make-up time) more than an hour or two lead is dangerous. Others may give up, thinking they will always be scooped.

9. Put thought into both the day of the week and the hour when scheduling a news conference. Pick what seems like a quiet day and hope that Syria doesn't decide to invade Israel and blow your story off the front page.

10. Sound bites! Prepare ten- or twenty-second statements designed to attract attention. Encourage the group spokesman to say something newsworthy in a unique, quotable fashion. This is a good research project for the brain trust. The importance of new, unique, hot quotes cannot be overemphasized.

11. When some of the media people fail to show up for a news event, immediately at the conclusion of the event hand-deliver a copy of the news release to anyone in the area who could not be there. Do this in person and be prepared to linger and talk if the request is made. The personal service will generate additional coverage next time.

12. Try diligently to use humor when responding to issues. Humor is a more important device when debating or sending letters to the editor but is extremely personalizing when used during a news conference. Humor is difficult to counter. Be careful, however, that you don't go overboard and appear flippant.

One-time, highly emotional issues such as a forced home school closing, the beating of nonunion workers, or the destruction of a citizen's home by agents of the Bureau of Alcohol, Tax and Firearms, are best captured for all posterity by members of the action group, by using video equipment. Necessary cameras even in the commercial three-quarter-inch format have come down in price so dramatically that groups that judge the device to be potentially effective should include it in their budget. Buy—and be prepared to use—the equipment if it is likely that the bureaucracy will attack.

Excellent video tapes of the bad guys violating the rights of men and women can be made and duplicated for wide distribution by the action group. TV people will invariably use the material if the production is halfway decent and the event is significant. Even radio people may review footage of the event and become so upset they give the event extra coverage.

Good videos can even become part of a traveling slide show to be taken around to Lions, Kiwanis and others.

People who are good with the media are invariably news junkies. They monitor every source to see what they are saying as well as what they are not saying. Going on with a monitoring program is very important for the successful Political Action Group. Without monitoring it is impossible to determine who among the media are doing a good job and who should be talked to.

In addition to one-on-one on the phone and occasional luncheon meetings, there are several devices that the shrewd news director can use to get a message to the media. One of the best is the press party. This is an informal event put together by the action group, which of course pays for the buffet and the booze.

Press parties are especially effective if the issue is a bit new or complex enough to benefit from extensive backgrounding. The freedom group should have several articulate, skilled speakers who can work the crowd.

Press parties are vitally significant when dealing with bureaucrats and their pals, who use smoke and mirrors to obscure their issue. Candidates sometimes use press parties when they find that their news conferences have degenerated into free-for-alls or they are mobbed by the media at speaking engagements.

When news conferences threaten to run out of control, an assistant must step in and announce an end to the questioning. This can be done by pointing out that it is 2:37, for instance, and we are overdue for the next meeting. "Please take one more question and then we must go," tell the spokesman—never scolding the media. Use this technique if the spokesman gets in over his head, is being ambushed, or finds himself speaking about issues of no relevance to those targeted by the Political Action Group.

At times one will encounter a truly obstreperous, lying, disruptive news person. It doesn't happen often but when it does and the person won't listen to reason or treat the group in a civil manner, there are a few devices the skilled media person can do to retaliate. (1) Do not invite the individual to any future news events. (2) Mention the person's unfairness to the news director in charge of the paper or station and make it clear that the offender will no longer be welcomed to the group's events. (3) Give the other media people exclusive stories that the offender is not privy to.

The media professional has three levels at which a story can be passed:

1. Exclusive interviews. This occurs when the group spokesman goes to the TV or radio station and gives that particular news person a private interview. These interviews must be used carefully, especially if the news person is called to the committee's office or is given news no one else has access to. Other media people become upset about being shut out if one is not careful when engaging in these types of interviews. Next time the group needs the media, they may not be particularly enthusiastic about showing up.

2. Remarks for the record. As a general rule, the group's speaker should make sure 95 percent of his remarks fall into this category. As the name implies, one is speaking with the intent of being quoted in this circumstance. Normal, run-of-the-mill news conferences fall into this category.

3. Off the record. This difficult and sometimes hazardous approach usually occurs when the group wants to pass information but does not want it attributed back to the spokesman. When the technique is used, the reporter will say "KGBK TV learned today that the home school group intends to personally sue the state teachers' union over the matter of the city closing home schools. Asked to confirm this report today, Jim Jones at the Home School Alliance said his group had 'no comment.'" Don't ever forget the commandment: There is no such thing as off the record. If you don't want to be quoted, don't say it.

A fourth category is called background. Its little brother is deep background. This type of interview is virtually never held with the group's spokesman, members of the brain trust, or other persons in charge. If it does take place, there should be a very clear understanding that what follows is exactly background information. The source will never be divulged, nor will stories be done quoting the speaker regarding the issue discussed. Only use this with trusted, proven reporters.

Use only background information techniques to give reporters the correct embarrassing questions to ask the opposition. Coach a smart secretary thoroughly and send her over to talk to a targeted reporter.

One of the most difficult situations occurs if freedom fighters are sufficiently successful to attract people from "20/20"- or "60 Minutes"-type programs. Apparently ambush interviews are no longer used by these people, meaning the interviewee will be called ahead for an appointment.

If your group is called, plan immediately to have a competent video cameraman there to record the entire interview for the Political Action Group. It is also wise to place a high-quality tape recorder in the room as a backup. If nothing else, the material is valuable later when preparing brochures and slide shows.

Handling the media properly is not a mystery, nor is it particularly difficult. It does, however, take forethought, ambition, and hard work. We must invest the necessary brain power to make the situation work for us.

Chapter 8

Writing News Releases and Doing Actualities

D oing a decent, readable, effective news release periodically during a campaign is essential. Our Side does not use them as often and as effectively as we could and this is curious. They are, of all the devices we might use, among the easiest and cheapest to construct.

News releases and actualities (see below) provide an often untapped opportunity to carry the attack into the enemy's camp at very short notice. We need to be more innovative in their use as to both frequency and basic construction.

The group should get out a news release for each press conference, speech and meeting. It should use news releases for anything that can get the group mentioned: when it wants to respond to a charge by the opposition, to make its own charges, to announce fund raising goals achieved, to announce the support of other organizations, to announce any changes in personnel, or for any other occasion that has some news value.

Be sure to mail releases to your opponents, especially if you mention them. In this case the release can simply state, "Jim Tyler, responding to comments about the United for Freedom Zoning Action Committee, said in West Chicago today that. . . ." Easy! Just the fact that freedom fighters are distributing a news release can throw the opposition off stride. Often the media will choose not to use the release, but the opposition won't know that for sure and will not want to take a chance. Their response, done in haste and confusion, can make them look shrill or silly. Bureaucrats hate adverse publicity so much that just knowing something is out there can ruin their bureaucratizing for days.

Humorous news releases and, if possible, news conferences are, in our opinion, a great untapped resource available to Our Side. Some freedom advocates argue that humor is inappropriate because of the perceived serious nature of the subject. The use of humor ducks serious debate on matters of great concern, they say. No question. These arguments are true as far as they go. They also make us look like colorless, unappealing, lemon-sucking sourpusses. Who will be interested in our cause if our leaders are not lively, friendly and human? Besides, humor is a wonderful tool with which to zap the Other Side if it *happens* to make a good point.

Writing releases is relatively easy because there are hundreds of real-life models available. Consult the local paper for a format.

The key rule for content is: *a release should have one and only one point.* The news editor must get the point from the heading, the lead and the entire release. So, reduce your message to a single, irreducible point and organize the release around that idea. The release should summarize the entire story in the first sentence or at most two. The lead should contain the classic five *W*'s: who, what, where, when and why.

Here's an example of an attention-getting lead:

West Chicago, January 15, 1988

Jim Tyler, speaking to a group of enthusiastic supporters, said today that a new action group had been organized to fight the unfair, dishonest, capricious and arbitrary actions of the Dupage County Planning and Zoning Committee.

Note the extensive use of buzz words to polarize readers (and let the news editor know that a fight is brewing). These draw immediate attention to group goals.

Print the release on the Political Action Group's letterhead. An original letterhead on good paper gives the impression the group is permanent, organized, determined, credible and professional. In many political action groups, news releases are the principal use of their bond letterhead.

Be careful that everything is spelled and punctuated correctly. No compromise here: everything must be English-teacher perfect. Antagonists enjoy using small grammatical errors to argue that we are an association of dolts.

On the upper left place the name of one or, if possible, two contact persons, including their phone numbers. They should be or become regulars with whom the media are used to dealing. If possible, the contact persons should be at the press conference and available later to answer phone questions as the story develops.

Below the names, place the date of the news conference or event you are announcing. Above the headline, below the letter-head block, give the release date of the document, either "For Immediate Release" or the date after which the material can be used.

Leaking the release must be done carefully and only with specific purposes in mind. The best situation can be leaking the release to the opposition bureaucrats if it seems unlikely that they can respond. Give them a copy a few hours before the news conference. When the media call, the opposition may plead "no comment, we haven't read the material." Your group can respond by saying, "That's curious. As a courtesy we gave them a copy of the material several hours ago!" Do not attempt to play these sorts of games with opposition groups that have talented spokesmen capable of coming up with a valid counter.

Work hard to make your headline riveting. It is the most important part of your release. Tell your story right there in the headline. Use active verbs. Avoid extraneous words and modifiers. Facts and figures speak more loudly than adjectives! Print the head in bold, upper-case letters. The point is to attract immediate attention. If the header isn't clear, topical and provocative, the editor won't read the rest.

News releases are best done on one page, but at times more is acceptable, especially if the release contains supporting items such as charts, graphs, pictures and financial analyses. Put the word "more" in parentheses at the bottom of the page of multiple-page news releases. On the last page put "(30)" at the bottom (journalistic shorthand for "the end of the document").

Use of the proper format goes a long way toward giving the group credibility it could not achieve so inexpensively by any other means.

Try, when developing the lead sentence, to think of a good *hook*. A hook is a journalistic term for an attention grabber that pulls the reader into the piece. Hooks are contained in the opening sentences, which also must give the reader most of the five *W*'s.

The next element in a news story is called a *bridge*. This is the sentence (or two) that carries the reader from the opening hook to the body of the article. Generally, if the writer is able to slip in a hot quote at this point, the bridge is livened up enough to carry the reader into the body.

Copy in the body of the release need not be extensive. It is basically used to document facts and figures not contained in charts and graphs attached to the news release and to draw the reader to the desired conclusions regarding the event.

Some writers use a series of questions asking, somewhat rhetorically, what the bureaucracy believes should be done about this important situation, etc.

News releases to be distributed at a press conference or some other event featuring a group speaker need not replicate the speaker's remarks. One or two or three powerful quotes from the speaker's prepared remarks work well. If the speaker is not using a prepared speech, you can frame the release about the subject to be addressed, paraphrase what the speaker is expected to say, develop group positions or arguments, or use quotations of what the speaker has said about this subject on other occasions.

Try in the body of the release to outline the speaker's and group's major emphasis and premise in a way that will jar the memory of the media people who attend the news conference.

News releases distributed at media events that have regional or national implications will be automatically filed with the wire services, by the major-media newsroom people. On seeing the story on the wires, national network TV may contact local affiliates for an update.

It is possible to attract network TV to news conferences, but only through local affiliates. Small local TV stations enjoy this type of opportunity. If they feel they are sitting on a story they are quick to get the word out. Political Action Group chairmen and spokesmen who develop personal relationships with local media people will quickly learn how the programs run locally and how to garner national coverage.

Our Side is quick to criticize the media when they do not cover our events. Often, however, our material is poorly prepared and presented by people who have not taken the time to determine exactly what kind of story excites the media people we are trying to attract.

Actualities

Professional press secretaries often get good mileage from a device called an *actuality,* which is all but unknown outside the broadcast industry. An actuality is a brief (ten to twenty seconds) recorded segment of the group spokesman's remarks, made available to the local radio stations for broadcast in a news spot. It can also be a video tape for television, but here we are concerned with radio spots.

Pick out a few really hot quotes that stand by themselves and that articulate the group's stand on an issue in a very few words. Examples: "We are disgusted with the State Board of Education's stand on home schools," and "If the Central Licensing Agency goes ahead with its published plan we won't have any place left to buy groceries or gas in our community."

Keep it short! No radio station we have ever worked with will use more than thirty seconds of material, and even that much is likely to get the story killed. On the other hand, it will nearly always use short, punchy quotes presented in a professional manner.

Pick out a sentence that is appropriate, recording it on a tape with a lead. The lead is composed of a brief announcement listing the speaker, date, place and event where the remarks were made. The remarks do not have to be live before an audience, but the sparkle achieved by using this format is obvious to radio people. The station news director will ask for these items when you call, but enumerating them a second time on the tape does no harm. At worst it gives the station time to adjust the audio on its end.

You can deliver the tape to the station (rush!) after phoning the news director. Or, if you're handy, you can send it over the phone from your recorder to his. That's tricky, to say the least: you have to string wires from the recorder to certain connections in the headset of the phone. Unless someone in the group knows or can learn exactly how to hook up the wires, hand delivery is safer if slightly slower.

Be sure the news director has your name and a phone number where he can reliably contact you for at least six hours.

Most smaller radio stations are one-man shows at a given moment. Anything that makes the job easier is appreciated. That is why a "wrapped" production can be the easiest way to get on the air. A "wrap" is a taped lead, followed by the voice of the news-maker (the actuality), then an out-tro (you guessed it—the opposite of an intro), and a sign-off. For instance: "Home schooler Mary Smith today said she was suing the school board for $1 million": [Mary Smith's voice]. [Announcer] "Smith said she expects to file the suit on Monday. This is Roger Rabner reporting from Reno."

A wrapped actuality allows the solo-broadcaster to plug your tape into the machine and play it for his broadcast. On a small enough station, sometimes our actuality *is* the newscast for two or three days. Big stations with real news departments won't bite on this bait. It's best to have your spokesman phone the station. It takes a little time, but you'll probably get on the air.

Radio lives and dies on actualities. Competition with other media will often incline a radio station to air your news when TV and the papers won't. Once the radio has carried it, you *are* news, so the other media editors may reconsider and run your release.

Sample News Release

For Immediate Release

Group Formed to Answer Planning and Zoning

Contact:
Paul Easter
(215) 312-7272 Office
(215) 302-8116 Home
John Nite
(215) 382-8371 Office
(215) 302-7718 Home

Property Owners' Group Accuses City of Illegal Taking
West Chicago, January 15

Jim Tyler, speaking to a group of enthusiastic supporters, said today that a new action group had been organized to fight the unfair, dishonest, capricious and arbitrary action of the Dupage County Planning and Zoning Committee.

"We named our group the Dupage Zoning Abolishment Program or DUZAP. And that's just what we're going to DO—ZAP unfair zoning," Tyler said. "It seems everyone I talk to is upset about this issue, and a lot of folks are joining our fight for our rights. We expect to have 400 members in another week or two. Clearly, the bureaucracy stepped over the line this time," he said.

"We are not going to sit quietly and surrender our freedoms," Tyler continued. "At the rate the group is growing, we will have enough financial muscle to both take the issue to courts and to organize a referendum," Tyler said.

"We intend to raise a minimum of $85,000 to use in our fight for freedom," Tyler said.

(30)

Chapter 9

Media Buyer

A ctive political groups may find they must resort to the purchase of radio, TV and newspaper ads. The media buyer's job is full of traps and hazards, so this is one time the group should turn to a professional, if possible. It is only too easy to waste money wholesale on ineffective ad placement. Perhaps a businessman or someone else in the group will have the necessary experience—by all means ask around. Otherwise, novices are going to have to do the job themselves. This is not desirable, but it does happen often enough. They'll have a lot to learn.

The work of placing media ads is terribly time-consuming and even more nerve-racking. The timing is intricate and the bucks are big. The buyer has to handle things just so or money raised a few dollars at a time from trusting donors will be lost forever, and perhaps the cause too. One is faced with the realization that a single goof, or at most two, can squander most of the group's precious media budget.

Great, long, authoritative books have been written on the subject of advertising, including media buys. If your group is faced with doing its own ad purchases, stock up at the library and learn all you can as fast as you can. This short chapter is not intended to take the place of more complete information or to give the novice the impression that he can easily handle this activity. It is intended to scare the newcomer into spending the literally hundreds of hours of study needed to learn the basics.

If at all possible, contract with an advertising agency to place the media spots on behalf of the group. Agencies receive a discount from the TV and radio stations and papers that effectively pays their fees. The process should cost no more than if the ads were placed by the group without outside help. Even by so doing, the group must exercise diligence in oversight. Many agencies, thinking that they are involved in a one-shot deal, will treat the project cavalierly.

Professional ad agencies should lay out a complete media plan, listing in detail where they feel the buys will be made, how much the buys will cost, why they are buying at the times suggested, and why they suggest the mix of media proposed.

Novice buyers should follow the same program if they do the job themselves. Start by going to all of the possible media in the region to request a rate card to find out how much the various vendors charge. Included with their rate card will be a demographic analysis of their viewer audience, listenership or readership. Beware of media that do not. They might be trying to sell you something totally unsuitable, such as spots at 4:00 A.M. or ones that have a teenage audience. Obviously, you want to put your ad in front of the kind of people who will be interested in your cause, and that's what the demographic profiles are for.

All major media can be evaluated on the basis of cost per thousand people reached as determined from their demographic sheets. Take the exact data with a grain of salt, but the relationships are usually valid.

Ask the various vendors about each other. Compare their data, their various claims and their claimed coverage. Reasonably intelligent people can do this, but it still is a swamp even at its very best. How does one compare, for instance, an ad on the 10:00 P.M. news costing $125 per minute with one run at 6:30 A.M. costing a bargain $35? It is never easy.

Also ask about production support. Groups with good, solid concepts can go to the radio and newspaper production department for assistance. However, do not even *think* about making television commercials in-house without extensive outside support. If you doubt this proposition, think back to the painfully amateurish TV commercials done years ago by auto dealers—customers stayed away in droves. Or think of home videos now.

Doing radio spots with a station's assistance may work fine till the spot is taken across town to a rival station having market segments not covered by the producer station. At that time the group may find that other stations refuse to run the spot using foreign announcers. It may be necessary to rerun the spot, using the second station's announcers at additional expense.

Once the word gets out that the group is spending for media, every schlock operator in the region will stop by to sell space on restaurant place mats, printed nail files, pencils, posters on city buses, sandwich boards, sky writing, and whatever else the fertile mind of *Homo salesmansus* can devise. (No, no, NO, you don't want any of these, they are useless for conveying a PAG's message.)

This is a good time to go back to the original group strategy and to the calendar developed early in the campaign. Evaluate the targeted groups that have a bearing on the project, as voters, or financial supporters or working foot soldiers. Stick to media that are "in character" for your group and its message to those whom it wants to reach. Stay away from the tricky advertising gimmicks, no matter what the salesman says. There is no such thing as reaching tens of thousands for pennies using nail files or embossed pencils. If there were, the soap companies would all be doing it.

The original plan and calendar should identify times when the group is holding news conferences, making statements, picketing, running letters to the editor, suing, sending out requests for money or whatever else. Integrate all purchased media into that schedule. Lay out a detailed calendar of suggested purchases with justification in writing—that helps everyone think it through—for each of the times and slots. Total up the budget and take this to the brain trust for evaluation.

A medium structured to reach an especially important group of potential supporters may be unusually expensive but nevertheless necessary. If there is no other method of reaching these people, then it must be done. Direct mail campaigning, for instance, has one of the highest costs per thousand but it does reach the elderly retired who tend to vote and to read their mail, but who may not listen to radio or watch TV.

Any media must be reinforced. This means that one ad may not do the job, but several coming from different sources will catch the person's attention. (In this regard, PAG media buyers should refer to the material on motivating people in chapter 14.)

Purchased media can be used in some cases for quick replies to charges made by the Other Side, or to handle shifting trends in public sentiment. Radio and TV are best for this but the lead time both for ad production and for placement are often hopelessly drawn out. Radio is faster and probably the best. Newspapers are never as fast as one would hope, and ads in print media have a reactive, undesirable look as well. Answering opposition charges is best done via news conferences or in press releases, if possible.

Billboards can be cost effective. They must be purchased months in advance, however; often before the issues are clear. Billboard advertising must be general and simple. The rule of thumb (because the people whizzing past don't have a chance to read much) is not more than seven words per billboard.

All advertising should have a built-in device for testing results. You have to know what results you are getting from each ad in order to invest your media budget well. Wherever possible, use a response device. This means having the ad ask people to *do* something (write, call an 800 number, send money), as opposed to merely asking for their support. Then put a code in the address or number they are to use so that you can identify which ad they are responding to, and count the responses. Make sure everything they "do" has an element that comes directly to the group. If you want supporters to write a legislator, for instance, have them send the letters or petitions to group headquarters, not to the statehouse, with the promise that the group will deliver the letters at a rally or with some other fanfare.

Here is an outline of the basic steps, for review:

1. Looking at what media may be needed.
2. Identifying what the campaign strategy calls for.
3. Asking the media for their rate and data information.
4. Developing a complete media plan including data for justifying each buy.
5. Staying away from the peripheral media quirks.
6. Matching the media plan with the campaign calendar and the strategic plan.

This is a complex undertaking that should not be approached by volunteers unless they have a great deal of time and dedication. If the job must be done in-house, assign just one person full time to buying media and to setting up news conferences.

Chapter 10

Budgets and Calendars

B udgets and a calendar of events based on the group's strategy provide a strong working plan for freedom fighters. Budgets are far more difficult to develop than the novice would suppose since, by nature, they reflect the philosophy and direction of the entire group. Calendars are relatively straightforward recitations of how the group feels events should unfold. Experience indicates that once the group does a strategy and a budget, the calendar is relatively easy.

Budgets are always tough because handling money takes a sharper focus than the sometimes vague philosophy that carries one into a project. You'll need to think through what your group is all about for the foresight to decide where the money will be spent and how it will be raised.

Do we, for instance, go after the opposition via radio, TV, newspapers, or not through the conventional media at all? If radio is the flagship for the group, will the station itself make up the spots? What coalitions can be formed? What about phone bills? Do we hire a spokesman/analyst? These and a thousand similar considerations run through the minds of political strategists at budget time, leading to more and more decisions. Any use of TV other than talk show participation will require the services of a professional. Putting expensive TV spots together must be done by a similarly expensive expert. To a certain extent, newspaper ad copy now falls into the same category. Billboards must be rented months in advance and are breathtakingly expensive. The foregoing are simplistic examples, but they do demonstrate areas where political action people are forced to sort things out when putting budgets together. Without putting figures in, here is a reasonable list of the categories which must be budgeted. This example is from a real campaign, larger than average:

Staff
Project director
Secretary
Precinct workers

Office Expenses
Letterhead, including design
Office rent
Utilities
Furniture rental
Computer rental w/printer
Copying
Postage
   (not including direct mail)
Office supplies
Dues & subscriptions
Office equipment purchase
Camera, film, processing
Phone
Phone hookup

Campaign Operation
Polling/poll
Mileage & travel
Fair booth
Meals & hospitality
Statistical analysis
Production of slide show
Meeting room/news conference
   sites
Photographer
Public relations agency retainer

Equipment
Video rental
Cassette recorder (purchase)
Phone answering machine
   (purchase)
Slide projector rentals

Campaign Materials
Posters
Direct mail brochures
Banners
Bumper stickers
Billboards
Fact sheets production & print
Lawn signs
Buttons
TV spots, write & produce

Direct Mail
Mailings by private canvassers
   (Note: If private carriers are
   not available, the cost per
   piece will go up to current
   third-class rates as set by the
   postal service)

Media Advertising
Newspaper/page
Radio/spot
TV

Miscellaneous

Let the brain trust perform the analysis necessary to put a budget together that the trust agrees has a 98 percent probability of carrying the day. From there we move on to a close, realistic look at the funding possibilities.

Raising money is an area all of its own. Many people cannot even make a ballpark stab at the amount they might collect. Admittedly it is painful but freedom fighters must give it their best shot. After a clear-eyed look at funding possibilities, the budget can be modified one way or another. Although it seems unlikely to newcomers to this business who are used to struggling along on very little money, there are times when the budget can even be expanded slightly, giving additional assurance of ultimate success. It also may develop that the original budget was an overkill that could safely be cut back without undue danger of losing the battle.

When, as is often likely, the budget must be cut, try to assign a probability factor to losing the whole campaign as a result of making particular cuts. Go through the list, cutting out what are considered to be the more expendable items. Good sharp polling will give the group information necessary to make these assessments.

The last thing to cut for most issues is the professional staff. These people bring new, innovative, professional approaches that are usually lacking among the original organizers. The only exception occurs when there is absolutely no money to pay support costs such as phone, office, secretarial, travel, etc. Volunteers can be organized but not nearly as well as one would hope or expect without paid professionals. This is advice that runs counter to conventional wisdom, but is eminently valid, in our experience.

In fund raising, hope for the best and avoid defeatism. Plan to raise enough money to succeed instead of setting forth with the tacit acceptance that you'll never raise enough. Quite a number of the budgeted items such as office space, stationery, printing, etc., could be donated. The budget is an excellent document with which to start fund raising. The rule for all political endeavors is to raise as much money as possible as early as possible.

One tip, when a sizable budget for television looks like a good target: those with the most TV—either paid or news commentary— will win. Large amounts in the media budget serve a dual purpose. Those who are spending with the media find that the newsroom covers their project much more thoroughly as well as less adversely. Given the choice, elect to put larger amounts of money in the media fund, knowing that papers and TV stations will occasionally switch or soften editorial policies as a result. The Political Action Group must still do tight, logical, defensible research and releases for the media, but by spending money with them, the news people may be more likely to maintain neutrality.

More than one freedom fighter has ponied up a preliminary budget that he has allowed to be leaked to the media. The technique has its dangers due to the operating philosophy it reveals. But to channel back the fact that large media buys may have a beneficial impact, especially in the case of relatively large purchases from relatively small stations.

One of the major keys to any budget's success is to set the miscellaneous budget high enough and then review expenditures at frequent intervals. During the throes of the campaign, it pays to compose a daily budget including changing estimates of various elements.

It is not unusual for some of the key players in the campaign to refuse to look at the financial information. The campaign manager must make up for the lapse by studying the finances daily so that valid recommendations can be made to the brain trust. Traditionally vendors require that all expenses be kept on a cash basis for any political endeavor. We have Mr. Gary Hart to thank for this development. Keeping the expenditures on a cash basis tends to prevent your financial situation from getting out of hand, however.

At the conclusion of the budgeting process, the organizing committee is usually so shellshocked that one virtually must talk about fund raising, thereby giving the group some reason for optimism. What is important at this time is knowing what resources are available to the group. The group should go through the broad categories of support that it will be looking to in the future including large gifts, direct mail, contributions in kind and others.

At that point, while everyone is still traumatized, make up a list of heavy hitters to whom the group might go for start-up money. Then list the various groups to whom the freedom fighters can appeal for funds. Funding from other groups takes inordinately long to come in. The real reason to start early with the groups is to secure their mailing lists for the freedom fighters' own use.

Along with public relations and the group's spokesman, raising money is a professional skill. Eventually the freedom fighters may wish to employ a paid professional on the group's staff. For the time being, knowing what lies ahead and having a workable plan that reflects the group's philosophy are important steps in the correct direction.

Once the big three—strategy, budget and calendar—are in place, the group is ready to start making waves.

Chapter 11

Strategic Philosophy

C itizens who organize to go to war with the bureaucracy must have an operating philosophy to guide the group's thinking and actions. Even combat has rules. The rules you go by should not only lead to victory, but maintain the group's character and integrity. Unless your operations are philosophically consistent, your troops will eventually lose heart and the group will fall apart.

Some of the traditional rules used by political activists are controversial among novice freedom advocates. At the top of that list is the truism that in political warfare the ends justify the means. There is no Geneva Convention in this business. We have to do whatever we can get away with or, more accurately, whatever the opposition will allow us to get away with, to win. This philosophy would be repugnant were we not engaged in recovering freedom that has been taken from us and is rightfully ours. It is much more understandable to troops who perceive that they have their backs against the wall. Freedom fighters like to assume that their basic freedoms are always guaranteed. They have to be shown that in the real world this is seldom true.

Once you establish that your cause is genuinely just and that you struggle against desperate odds, things get simpler. Those who are dedicated, experienced, clever and perhaps tricky will prevail. Few of the warriors on Our Side fit into this category today, principally because the bureaucracy is smart enough not to present us with black and white "your-back-is-against-the-wall" choices. This may help explain why we so seldom feel real concern about losing freedom, to the point that we'll fight to get it back.

48

As a practical matter it is nearly impossible to predict when people will become so incensed that they elect to wage all-out war. We can say that, at this writing, many citizens are approaching this point over the abortion issue, property taxes, federal confiscation of resources, and local planning and zoning.

Some of the rules discussed below may be too radical for the average freedom fighter. We include them for informational purposes, hoping things are never so bad that they must be used.

Actually, more experienced political activists tend not to be as militant as newcomers who initially feel that anyone not with them is against them and is thus "no damn good." You have to beware of such political kamikazes! Their tendency is to take no prisoners and amass power till the pursuit of it becomes an end in itself. But power is the enemy. Power tends to corrupt and it will corrupt Our Side as easily as it does the Other Side. Group leaders should keep a tight rein on operations lest they become fanatical. Allow plenty of flexibility in plans and go after the strength in numbers rather than ideological purity. People have different degrees of intensity on an issue. Some will follow along with the parade if it is not required that they be especially vocal or strident.

Be especially flexible when building coalitions. Politics does, indeed, make strange bedfellows. Our Side must learn to operate on the concept that a class of people may be wrong about this or that issue but are never totally "no damn good" as human beings. We can make common cause on *our* issues.

Freedom fighters will operate to their own self-interest. On the other hand, because a bureaucrat works for the government—i.e., all the people—he may be clothed with more perceived self-righteousness than is warranted. All of us are presumed to be fair, honest and even-handed but in real life this is seldom true.

Expect even our people to go with the group on an issue only if it ultimately serves their own self-interest. Bureaucrats universally believe they are supporting a cause that is unselfishly in the best interests of "all of society" and they are just about universally wrong in this. We can't let them clothe themselves with a righteous air of being above us because they are part of the government. They are no more fair, honest and noble than anyone else. On the contrary, big government is the problem. Those who work within its faulty system should be held responsible precisely for their honesty when they are trying to hide behind The Rules.

Because humans working on a freedom project know they are operating on shaky ground when they act selfishly, they will seldom be up front about admitting to their own selfish motivation. Wise group leaders look beneath the layers of camouflage and rhetoric in an attempt to discover why both supporters and detractors are acting as they are.

A Chinese proverb says that one should never attempt to break a person's rice bowl (destroy his means of livelihood). While this explains why some bureaucrats act as they do when their program or office is under attack, it should not deter dedicated freedom fighters. We need have no misgivings about sending bureaucrats and politicians back to honest, private employment. It is, let's say, ever a useful learning experience for them to have to earn a living under the same discipline the rest of us do, in the marketplace.

When developing a strategy, continue to look for flexibility and angles that aren't obvious, but always treat the issue before both the public and one's supporters as completely obvious and utterly black and white. Supporters rally poorly to an uncertain bugler. Likewise, never be deterred from the original objective. Staying on course in the face of skillful counter-strategists is never easy.

Be sensible about using the resources available. No matter what the group does, assuming it is halfway effective with it, the opponents will, when their suffering starts, accuse your side of unethical behavior, including trickery. This is reason enough not to employ anything that even hints of underhandedness if you have the resources to do anything better.

Several years ago Larry Grupp ran a political project in a medium-sized city. One of the staff, a lady with exceptional clerical abilities, was also incredibly clever. She often got more than her share of the office work completed early, then she sat around thinking of tricks to play on the opposition. Some of her ploys were absolutely brilliant. Most bore no relationship to the campaign, serving only to harass peripheral opposition players. It is doubtful if these people could have ever seen the relationship between our activities and their own misfortune, had we implemented this lady's suggestions. Larry's toughest duty was to ride herd on the lady's fetchingly fertile imagination. We were never in great danger of defeat, nor were we operating on such a shoestring that we needed anything but straightforward political tactics. There was, in short, no reason to depart from our solid winning strategy, and reason not to in the chance, however slight, that our trickery would be discovered.

Be particularly cautious that, in one's drive to be innovative and questioning, one's supporters and workers are never asked to do something they are incapable of. Farmers call this "expecting a pig to fly." Volunteer workers can be developed and taught. Many will, out of sheer modesty, disclaim abilities that, in fact, they have. The campaign chairman, supported by the brain trust, must learn to separate the cream from the milk in this regard.

A painful example of asking people to be something they are not occurs when the group achieves enough notoriety to attract TV coverage. Down-home, inexperienced freedom fighters must never be thrown into a TV news show setting unless they have been coached extensively in advance. The only exception is when the strategy calls for a sympathy-getting event in which your group seemingly, by accident, participates in an amateur sort of way and is mercilessly raked by the media. Otherwise, pick a strategy that fits the talents and capabilities of individuals in the Political Action Group. Make sure your most articulate people field the hostile media questions, not the rank and file. If necessary, hire professionals or call in experts.

This philosophy has an important flip side. Insofar as possible, force the bureaucrats to operate outside areas of their expertise. Orchestrate it so they find they must call in experts. Do this by being innovative and framing a strategy so unexpected that they have little background against which to deal with it. Make them get out from the safety of their office cubicle to go on TV, attend acrimonious hearings unprepared, face hostile groups of citizens, respond to critical letters to the editor, editorial comments and questions from their superiors. Waste their time, energy and money going to court answering lawsuits, and so on.

Politicians running for office refer to this syndrome as taking the high ground—i.e., making one's opponents continually react to the group's efforts in a manner which is odious to them or concerning which they are unfamiliar and unprepared. If the bureaucracy cannot cope with the tactic and falters even briefly, the battle is won.

Two of the most potent day-to-day methods of stepping out-side the comfort zone of the average bureaucrat are (1) to employ humor and (2) to learn the agency's rules and regulations better than the agency people themselves. Better still, do both at once. Hang them with their own rope and then laugh at them.

Humor is wonderfully destructive to bureaucrats. It leaves them spluttering, with no firm issue or ground to respond. Our Side, unfortunately, tends to be too sour and humorless. We bear the brunt of the regulator's barbs in silence or so resentfully that we can do nothing but complain. If we see bureaucracy as the eternal bumbling idiocy it is and stop taking it so personally, we can draw some of its sting with laughter and jeers.

Political activists with sharp researchers in their group should set these people to work immediately learning the rules and regu-lations of the bureaucracy with which they are at war. Good, painstaking research will pay large dividends in tying up the bureauc-racy with its own rules. This function is not easy nor is it quickly implemented. By campaign's end some members of the group should have become experts on the bureaucracy with which they were at war.

Our counterparts—believers that enough regulation will change society to their own utopian dream—are masters at this concept. They ferret out the weak spots, grab the bureaucrats' own rules and summarily hang them around their necks like a dead turkey. In the long run their stratagems usually work, because no matter how much they may embarrass or harass bureaucrats, increased regula-tion means more bureaucrats, and more work for them.

Whatever strategy is employed, be certain that it allows for con-tinuously escalating pressure on the opponents. A hit now and then, done in a desultory, piecemeal fashion will almost never be suc-cessful. Seasoned political fighters refer to this continuous pressure as "building." Effective campaigners must build day by day, always upping the ante, always positively.

Chapter 12

Influencing Partisan Politicians

Redirecting the philosophy of campaigning candidates for office is almost criminally easy compared to influencing them after they are safely elected and entrenched in office. Candidates simply cannot overlook citizen groups floating around with unappropriated issues. They migrate philosophically toward fresh issues as instinctively as geese flying north in spring. All your PAG has to do is make its new cause known, loud and clear, and candidates will soon be assimilating your program, ultimately espousing your views as their own.

Consider. Norman Thomas first ran for president of the U.S. on the socialist ticket in 1928. By the time he was finished in 1944, he had run a total of five times. Never did he get as many as one million votes. When he quit it was not because he was discouraged or he felt his cause was hopeless. He quit because he no longer had any issues on which to run. Every one of his platform planks had been passed into law by the major parties!

Political candidates' need for viable issues can be exploited by almost any PAG. The real trick is getting the group organized into a tenacious, fighting unit. Successful political activists must spend most of their initial time and energy organizing their followers. Organizers will need to issue statements, send out newsletters and hold news conferences, knowing that if they perform well, a politician will quickly swoop in and claim them and their issues for his own. The following are approaches the new Political Action Group can take to influence political campaigns.

A primary requirement is a list of demands. Call it what you will: a goal, platform, charter, political agenda; but it must be widely publicized and well known to all players. These demands are the considered, seasoned goals which originally brought the group together. Expect to devote a lot of quality time and thought at the outset to deciding *exactly* what the group wants. The political wish list should be pondered, brainstormed, debated, refined, given to the brain trust for critique, and pondered again. When it is purified and polished, a coherent statement of goals and objectives should be written with the greatest care, and published. These are your demands and they are the strategic extension of the goals set out at the start of the campaign. Circulate the statement to all of your workers so that the rank and file understand the situation.

Publicizing your objectives will force underdog, inexperienced politicians who are searching for a constituency to consider these goals in a helpful way. Norman Thomas won his objectives by simply articulating his views and running a determined, visible race for president, though the average citizen thought his chances hopeless.

The size of the PAG dictates its reach. The objectives of little groups are swallowed up by local political interests while medium-sized groups attract state politicians. Grow large enough and the national politicians will be there knocking at the group's door. The Right-to-Lifers are a good, contemporary example.

It is the nature of a democracy that we need to understand and manipulate to our advantage. The group's membership numbers and its published goals are what count, not the fact that it can sweep a friend into office. Without a similarly organized countervailing group, the issues are a shoo-in for adoption given a few years and the ability of the group to keep itself organized.

Political Action Groups that elect not to wait for the politicians to come to them have two fairly difficult tasks ahead of them. Assuming they have organized and published a list of objectives, they must then go the next step and pick a candidate who (1) will agree to carry their water and (2) can win the election. Should it be impossible to combine these two elements, the authors strongly urge that the group spend additional time on other fronts such as perfecting the organization, slide shows, fact sheets, raising money, newsletters and harassing bureaucrats, all the while waiting for the politicians to come to it.

It is vital that the group pick a candidate who can win. Because winning on the issues is a necessity, it is important that an endorsement for any candidate be withheld early in the group's existence. Let enough time pass before endorsement so that winnable, seasoned politicians can evolve into philosophically supportive positions.

Many groups foolishly jump into races too early, supporting first-time candidates who are so amateurish or carrying so much bad baggage that they cannot possibly secure popular approval. This is unfortunate since it cripples the group's credibility at a time when wounding can be mortal.

The really difficult task for the political organizer is to convince the group that it might have to accept a candidate who may not be completely pure on its issues, but who can win. Most groups intuitively wish to endorse a candidate who is solid on every issue; but the important concept is to pick someone solid on issues of immediate concern who has more than a remote chance of winning. Discontent is all but guaranteed when the brain trust analyzes whom to support. Waves of disagreement can sweep through the group at this time, threatening to tear it apart.

Supporting acceptable standing candidates out of the clear blue is easy and fun. When polls show that a person has a clear lead, and you know that person is sold on your issues—and when you are certain that you can make good on it—call the campaign staff and say that you have, say, twenty-five volunteers ready to go door to door passing out the candidate's literature. If the candidate says, "Okay, cover River City for me," you have two immediate considerations. First, like it or not, your issues have become his issues. Let it be. Some in your group may feel proprietary toward the issues they raised and developed, but let the candidates have all the credit they want. They need the credit and it locks them into doing what you want. Second, you will find that you must now crack the whip over your group mercilessly so the troops perform as promised. Maintaining discipline at this point can be extremely difficult.

At this point there is no choice: the group leader must physically deliver the group of workers to the candidate's office or out to the meeting place in the precinct *en masse*. Asking one's foot soldiers to show up on their own does not have nearly the impact of delivering a throng of people ready to work. If possible, use buses or mini-vans to deliver the group. Be sure at the start that if the group agrees to provide twenty-five volunteers for four hours, that is actually the number that shows up. Not achieving as promised drops the group's credibility immeasurably. Don't promise more "warm bodies" than you can deliver.

In preparation the group should consider holding a news conference explaining to the media that it intends to go door to door for the candidate. If the PAG's agenda is thought to be a bit radical or unusual, it is sufficient at this time to say we agree with the candidate's stand and we intend to help. This works even if the candidate has not publicly stated that the helping group's issues are his or her issues. If the group is held together and if the group agenda is well known, the candidate has, by accepting the group's public help, accepted its issues as his own.

The authors can assure you from experience that this seemingly simple act of organizing a work party for a candidate is a thousand times more effective both for the candidate and for the group than a straightforward news conference endorsement. It has always been a mystery why political groups even do formal endorsements when they could orchestrate something far more effective for the candidate's immediate needs.

Other groups have often been effective at using endorsement conferences to snap candidates into line, that is, making them pay for the endorsement. They ask those standing for election to appear before a panel made up of group members. At the conference the candidates are grilled regarding their past performance and possible future stands on issues. Rank and file members of the group are invited to participate as members of the audience. After meeting the candidates, listening to their statements and quizzing them, the group generally votes on endorsements. The League of Women Voters has brought this lobbying device to a fine art.

Political Action Groups that are polling have an attractive resource to offer politicians. Politicians will figuratively drive their pickups over their mothers' backs to secure the results of a recent, reasonably competent poll. Regional and even local polls are expensive. They are seldom done by state and local candidates. Of course the group would not be talking to a candidate unless its own poll already showed a good chance for a victory. As a practical matter, polls should not be mentioned to politicians the group does not want to identify with.

On many occasions, we have tracked, or worked closely with, candidates who were running for state and national seats. After a few weeks of cooperation with our people carrying their literature, they actually started carrying our material. Instead of their moving over to usurp our campaign, we took over their campaign. At one time, using several politician's volunteers, we were covering a city of 120,000 with our issue-oriented literature every two weeks, saving a huge direct mail budget.

Eventually, alert candidates running for elected office will ask for the group's mailing list. This will usually happen between the time the volunteers show up and the time the group formally, openly endorses the candidate. The list should *not* be given free lest it be construed as a political contribution that might cause legal problems.

But other, more pressing issues confront the brain trust relative to releasing its mailing list. Will the candidate, for instance, use the list in an attempt to mail literature to influence votes or will he or she use the mailing list to try to raise funds? Assuming the group has been doing its own fund raising in a professional, thorough manner, as well as keeping the members informed, the results from soliciting the members yet again for money, or from a letter appealing for political support, may be minimal. Your group won't look good if the politico does not even get back the price of postage. Another serious problem, if the group's information net is not working well, is that group members may be privately offended by the request, which seems to come out of the blue. Informed members may take a ho-hum attitude about receiving another request for funds, but they may be upset that their names were released. There are few hard, fast rules for releasing mailing lists, so evaluate on a case by case basis.

Besides workers, polls and mailing lists, the group has other items of value to offer. As mentioned in chapter 23, on newsletters, an offer to publish a candidate's views in the house organ can be most enticing to a candidate. The group can do some organizational chores, and the brain trust might provide guidance on the handling of some issues.

Dealing with Elected Officials

After election the political arrogance factor goes up immeasurably. Then one must go to the legislator with hat in hand. The formula for meeting person to person with legislators is conventional, not having any of the elements of influencing them before they are elected.

Meeting with legislators over certain issues can be tough. Basically the same rules apply at all levels of government. They have evolved into a formula:

1. Make an appointment ahead for a specific time that works well for the group spokesman and for the legislator. After calling the legislator's appointments secretary, it is wise to confirm in writing if circumstances warrant.

2. At the initial call, let the office staff know why the appointment is being made. At every level, legislators work very hard at making you believe they are the smartest people on earth and certainly don't want to appear to be ignorant regarding an issue. They will expect their staff to brief them thoroughly on the pros and cons of your cause before you arrive in their offices. They can't do that if the purpose of your visit is a mystery.

3. Make sure you are going to see the correct person. This may take some professional advice. In many cases the wrong guy is targeted. Then the group plays the "Oh-sorry-it's-not-me-see-Joe-down-the-hall" game. When you go to see Joe, he is out for six months.

4. Try, if at all appropriate, to schedule a luncheon or dinner when it will be easier to sit down and discuss issues at length. This is especially useful when dealing with complex issues that do not lend themselves to a quick yes or no. Be prepared to buy grits for one or more legislators' assistants under this plan.

   The group treasurer should be forewarned that these events can run into money.

5. Be absolutely proper about being on time for the meeting. Dress correctly and bring along only those you have told the receptionist will be in the party. At one time in the past, we included a very well known, near celebrity in our group at the last moment. The legislator was thrown off stride by the dignitary's presence—not a good way to secure a legislator's cooperation.

6. Local and state legislators are always relatively easy to see, provided they want to be met with. However, some of us live 2,000 miles from our national congressmen. Getting to Washington, D.C., can be difficult and is always expensive.

   Congressmen all come back home on a fairly regular schedule. They come to fairs, hearings, town meetings, party rallies, fund raising dinners and receptions and many other functions. At the time they will usually agree to meet with representatives from your group. It may be weeks, however, till the meeting actually takes place. This is not an acceptable plan if the potential loss of freedom is imminent.

   Demonstrating that the issue is important to the group is vital. Committee people who travel long distances to meetings with their legislators demonstrate their seriousness. Agreeing to a 6:00 A.M. breakfast or a meeting held late at night may accomplish the same when the meeting is scheduled on one's home turf.

7. In most cases, expect the meetings to be very brief. Ask those in your delegation not to sit down or otherwise make themselves comfortable. People who both dress properly and remain standing for a meeting have much more presence than those who handle their affairs more casually, especially if they give the impression they are there for business and not to camp in the legislator's office.

   If the congressman seems preoccupied during the meeting, it is probably because he or she is trying to figure out whether your project represents too many voters to be ignored or so few that they can safely be written off. The permanence and good organization of your group are a plus.

8. If the meeting is held near home, be creative about accepting suggestions regarding a place to meet. Legislators spend hour upon hour upon hour at boring cocktail parties, socials, ban-

quets and others. Often they will happily devote some of this time to discussing significant issues provided they can remain bodily at the function and you agree to tag along.

9. Be prepared to support your case with extensive charts, graphics and data. Extensively researched, in-depth fact sheets, efficiently summarized, make a good impact. If the group has slides or photos, take these along. Bring any special video players or other equipment you need to the legislator's office. Never assume or believe the receptionist who tells you they have the necessary equipment and that it works. At the end of the meeting, leave a one-page written summary of your points with the legislator. If the group can see at the time only an aide, by all means do the presentation for the aide. Aides usually influence their bosses far more than the boss will ever want to admit.

10. Do not assume that a legislator is automatically for or against your program. Invariably this decision will be made later, on the basis of how many potential votes are at stake.

    Commitments regarding the issue are seldom given at the first meeting unless the issue contains elements of a campaign promise that the group can, by some creative means, recall to the legislator. Only novice legislators will box themselves in with a firm commitment and that will probably not prove to be truly firm in the future.

    When pressed, most legislators will give a general indication of support or opposition, thickly lathered with qualifying provisions.

11. One of the most often neglected skills helpful when meeting legislators is the ability to listen to what is really being said. Legislators on all levels enjoy giving people The Word, expecting them to stand quietly listening to their wisdom.

    Doing this successfully requires that we walk a very fine line between genuinely listening, allowing or not allowing him or her to avoid the issue, stroking the person's ego, and actually getting the job done. Be forewarned.

12. In every regard, do not neglect to pay courtesy calls on legislators whenever you are in town. An amateur could become a reasonably successful lobbyist by simply calling on legislators over and over with nothing more to say than "Hello, how are you?"

When they are in, say "Hello. I am [whatever] from the River City Political Coalition" and let it go at that. When (more often) the legislator is not there, leave a card and go on to the next office. After two months of this routine, one could go in and ask for a vote on virtually any issue and at least be taken seriously.

13. Try to be sensitive to legislators' needs on the issue. If they indicate more research is needed, do it quickly. If supporting mail from home is needed, get it to them pronto. When talking to a legislator outside the group's district, an offer to move resources into that person's district in support of a campaign on one's position may be effective.

Never arrive late, fail to listen, talk too long yourself, misrepresent the true situation or use factoids on legislators. Dress appropriately and never go storming in as if you were going to collect land rent from the devil. The legislator may be the devil himself but hostility seldom does the group any good.

It takes more care, feeding, money and time, but legislators can be influenced after they are safely ensconced in office, especially if one will do the necessary background on an issue and couch the arguments so as to appeal to that individual legislator. The brain trust must decide if this is the best, most effective method of getting the job done.

Chapter 13

Changing Laws

W̲e are impressed by the printed word—sometimes too much. We tend to believe that once an item appears in print it is final, and once a law is written it is carved in stone. Nothing could be further from the truth.

New legislators on the local, state or national level are usually surprised (and disgusted) to find that fully one third or more of their time is spent rewriting inappropriate legislation. Laws are finicky things and usually have unexpected and politically unpleasant consequences. Every legislative body spends much time on "oversight," amending or undoing its previous mistakes. A large part of new legislation is correction of old legislation.

That gives hope and opportunity to PAGs trying to change a bad legal or regulatory situation. So note well: *laws and regulations can be changed.* Freedom fighters must thoroughly believe this or remain impotent when dealing with legislative and regulatory matters.

Knowing the Law

The very first thing to do when told by a bureaucrat that a freedom is "against the law" is to ask, "Which law?" Tell him you want to see it in black and white. Be specific, friendly and firm. Insist on seeing chapter and verse. In most cases, bureaucrats are extremely happy to oblige. In their world, anything and everything in writing is gospel.

After giving you the code section under which they operate, you will probably be given a list of departmental regulations. On the national level a citation will be made setting out the date they were published in the Federal Register. This is the point at which the Political Action Group should become intensely skeptical. Things may not be as the bureaucrat represents them. Huge amounts of critical research should be undertaken at this point.

The brain trust must evaluate the interpretation and enforcement of the code section, especially as it relates back to rules the agency is promulgating. Ask why this "thing" is being enforced now and not two months ago. Be absolutely sure the group knows who is enforcing the rule and why. Is it state, local or federal law one is dealing with? At times local officials will say that enforcement is mandated by federal law; smart manipulators will diligently inquire into the truth of this statement.

It may be helpful to secure qualified legal help to determine if recent case law supports the position taken by the bureaucracy. An attorney may be asked to volunteer his or her services, but experience indicates that good attorneys who fight regulatory infringements on freedom do not volunteer to the extent of those who favor government intrusion. Therefore, you must expect that good advice must be paid for. The group may have to hire the required attorney. Rather than ask him or her to volunteer, ask for a donation of money to the group that is then used as his fee.

An ideal task for volunteers is doing legal research on the issue. This is surprisingly easy and can save the group fees that an attorney would normally assess. Usually the research must be done under the direction of the attorney, who is also paid for this supervisory time spent on the project.

Using the group attorney, you can make requests of other attorneys who have previously done research on these sorts of matters. Don't overlook going to other Political Action Groups that have already been down this path, at least in part.

A very simple expedient that is overlooked with maddening frequency by Our Side is to ask the state attorney general for his opinion on state and local issues. It may take the signature of a state legislator on a letter written by the political group to get the attorney general to act, but it is the rare legislator who won't go at least this far, even if he is basically opposed to what the group is doing.

The Bureaucratic Role

Great numbers of bureaucratic mandates are developed and written by agencies that have the duty of interpreting the intent of the laws passed by the legislature. In most cases the legislators will pass laws having little idea how the agencies will enforce them. The first signs of trouble occur when the legislators hear complaints from their constituents who are abused by the regulations.

At this point it is extremely important to remember again that the Political Action Group must go after every scrap of information it can; there's no such thing as too much information. Many a time a PAG has been helpless simply because it didn't know enough about which statute or departmental regulation was causing it grief. The existence of case law, departmental rulings and prior legal action never entered into these defeated freedom fighters' minds.

Another excellent information-gathering technique is determining when the statute in question was enacted. Use this date to look up the original testimony that was given in support of the measure including legislative input showing intent of the measure. This information is helpful when building a case saying the bureaucracy has overstepped its legislative mandate.

If the statute is plainly misinterpreted, freedom fighters have several excellent courses of action. They can make it a media event, they can sue or they can quietly work to change the law or the agency chief, or start an effort to do away with the department's funding. All of these are viable.

Should the problem prove to be an especially irritating bureaucrat who is overstepping his bounds or his authority, give serious thought to implementing a *Moose Jaw* strategy. Moose Jaw is government slang for being transferred to some remote office in a horrible place. It is nearly impossible to fire bureaucrats, but they can be reassigned. The threat of moving them to a humble post does get their attention.

Another good strategy is to go to the funding authority with a serious, well considered plan to cut the offending agency's budget severely. This has been done successfully at almost every level of government, from building inspectors to state universities to federal agencies.

At times the threat of a lawsuit will cause bureaucrats to straighten up and fly right. As with all political action projects, the fear of doing a thing is greater than the thing itself. This is true in spades when dealing with bureaucrats, who as a class are often fearful, reticent people who hate legal action. This rule—threatening them with exposure or risk—also applies to lobbying, picketing, holding news conferences, and any other political activity that puts them in the public eye.

Another similar hard and fast rule applies in this case. Never, ever threaten that an action will be taken and then not do it. To be sure, it's fun to threaten bureaucrats but it's absolutely a no-no if there is any chance the group is incapable, organizationally, morally or financially, of carrying through on its threat.

Better to operate the other way: sit down with bureaucrats and tell them quite candidly and matter-of-factly that you are thinking of legal action. On returning to your office, call the attorneys and tell them to file. Speak softly and carry a big stick. The next time you express concern to a legislator or bureaucrat, he may respond more cooperatively.

At times raising a stink helps. Even a very small group can get that job done. There is a rule of stinks, however: A stink might change rules, but major revisions such as changing whole code sections require different, more sophisticated methods. The group may elect to start making life miserable for bureaucrats, taking every opportunity to point out to a bureaucrat's superiors that he is demonstrably unable to get along with the people he is supposed to serve. In the case of middle management types, this sort of effort is incredibly easy to orchestrate. Laws won't change, but rules and regulations might magically disappear or lapse into non-enforcement.

Changing a Law

If in the end a PAG is unable to get its situation eased by pressure, and when it is certain that the law stands against its ends, the group will have to move to the next stage and make plans to change the law. This is the toughest road, but still possible. Much of the remainder of this book is dedicated to giving practical instructions on how to carry the battle to the appropriate body. Always remember, a year or two is not a very long term, and that laws can be changed.

One avenue may be easy. Small changes in laws done as part of an oversight function generally draw little attention. Legislators don't much care for this drudge work and like to stick newcomers with the chore. A friendly legislator working on revisions of law can sometimes get your job done by changing a word or two. A "may" might be inserted for a "shall," or such similar device. Voilá, the law's teeth are pulled. Junior legislators can pull this sort of thing off if they are bright enough to learn the system.

Changing actual laws virtually always requires the sympathetic cooperation of an elected official in the legislative body in which the measure was originally enacted. At times, old long-standing organizations such as education associations, farm bureau associations, contractors' associations, etc., can push through specific legislation without using a specific legislator. This happens only because they understand from long experience who their elected friends really are. Many put money into a number of different—even opposing—campaigns, expecting recipients to carry their water later on if the need arises.

Newly formed Political Action Groups developed for a specific purpose may find they must spend quite a bit of time and money looking around for a legislator friend who will help them.

Sometimes it is more reliable, though also more expensive, to breed and raise your own politician. It has been done before. Creating a group candidate is not the best course of action, but sometimes it is unavoidable, if the matter cannot be left to the lottery of normal political process. Start far enough back in the process that you can bring forward the candidate, gussy him up by teaching him to speak and dress correctly and run him with the intention that he handle a single bill. That person will seldom run on a platform that openly and consistently includes the fact that this specific bill is high on his agenda. As a general rule, in most elections voters couldn't care less about these detailed issues.

This technique has several obvious problems and several that are not so obvious. At best this is a relatively long-term solution to the problem. The technique can be expensive and relatively uncertain since a seat on the targeted governing body may not be readily available. Old, entrenched city councilmen or commissioners, for instance, may continue sitting till the pallbearers come to get them. Once elected, our person will require the close support of knowledgeable people regarding the way laws are written, introduced and passed in that jurisdiction, matters usually beyond a legislative novice. Providing this staff support is expensive. Political Action Groups too often feel they have done their job getting that person elected, then fade from the scene before the job is really finished. They must continue to stand with their elected official.

Alternatively, finding a candidate who will run with the understanding that an offending law will be changed for the group is thought to be difficult, but isn't. Unless the contest is in a large city such as Chicago or a large state such as California where huge amounts of money are needed to run, a candidate will invariably surface. There are just too many people with big egos floating around to ignore the lure of group support when running for office. The real problem is finding one that is winnable.

In the unlikely event there are no viable candidates, the group should try talking to incumbent legislators about their problem. Legislators, especially those with primary contests, are more easily influenced early in the election process. It is often amazing what can be done by sitting down with the candidate a month before the campaign opens.

It is a hard and fast rule that as to money, time and expert input, the easiest time for an opposition candidate to run is in a weakly contested primary. Political Action Groups with their bloc of votes wield much power in low-turnout primaries. Incumbents are greatly and perhaps unrealistically paranoid about primary competition.

Incumbents locked in tough races can often be heavily influenced before election. Try calling off the committee so as to defuse an issue for a brief time, and then go to the candidate with the offer of financial and bloc vote support. If possible, go to several candidates with an offer of support. This procedure must be handled with a great deal of finesse. Candidates locked in a tough race will promise almost anything as long as it does not impinge on their moral values or past promises.

Remember, rules can always be changed with relative ease. Laws take a bit more planning, including a long-term strategy, but they also can be changed. We say again, when Our Side learns to believe this, it can get out and make a difference.

Chapter 14

Motivating People to Vote

Two general classes of voters interest political manipulators. These are legislators, who vote on laws; and citizens, who vote for the legislators. The two kinds of voting may not seem similar, but both can be analyzed with the same sort of tools. We therefore discuss both here.

The issue of accurately predicting why certain legislators will vote in predetermined patterns is especially important for those who are working to persuade legislators to vote in acceptable free-market patterns. Political Action Groups looking for a citizen who will agree to stand for election want to be reasonably certain that their person will carry their water later, or when their key bills start coming up. It isn't ever easy but a formula does exist.

Accurate foreknowledge as to how citizens are likely to vote is similarly important. Assuming the Political Action Group intends to put forward a new candidate, it is reassuring to have some formula by which it can gauge the person's consistency and electability. Understanding and predicting voting patterns are much easier than most novice Political Action Groups would even suppose. Influencing these same voters to go along with the group's initiative program is always tough, but is—of course—somewhat easier when the system is understood. The following is the simplified analytical breakdown that public opinion pundits have successfully used for years.

Evaluating Legislators

Legislators generally vote as a result of three core influences. Now and then a maverick will come along; people will say, "It's crazy, we never know how he will come down." But the rules apply to nearly all of them.

The first, easiest area to predict is the body of legislation or rules that impinges on the long-held moral views of the person involved with them. An excellent example of this type of issue is asking a devout Roman Catholic to vote in favor of abortion on demand. Other issues in this category might include pornography, or perhaps zoning a bar within a thousand feet of a school or church. Moral issues are often fueled by religious fervor. Most people determine their morals not with their minds, but with their hearts, in line with traditional family, church and community values. When we know that the issue has or can be made to have moral overtones and we know the moral underpinning of the legislator, we also know exactly how that person will react.

But, contrary to popularly held opinion, legislators very, very seldom get to vote on issues that touch on their traditional beliefs. Seasoned legislators estimate that moral issues affect 1 to 2 percent of the bills they vote on. For purposes of discussion and understanding, 5 percent is a maximum value falling in this category.

On this type of issue there is absolutely no sense in trying to convince the person to vote contrary to his moral persuasion. People who persist in doing so, even when the legislator listens politely, will lose enough credibility that they will not be welcomed back a second or third time. The best course of action is to know the legislator well enough so that one does not go in with a request that will be viewed as immoral.

The second type of issue relates to campaign promises made during the heat of battle. The general public is often surprised to discover how cautious legislators are about keeping campaign promises.

Elected public officials generally develop their positions (the things they promise) on the basis of surveys of their constituency. They want to know what is on the electorate's mind so that they can come up with the appropriate promises in the appropriate way.

By so doing they expect to be hired by the voters. It is usually futile to try and convince a legislator to take a stand in opposition to one taken publicly and openly during a campaign. Or worse, one loses credibility trying.

Casual observers would suppose that this type of issue constitutes most of what a legislator busies himself with during his term in office. Actually, legislators have little opportunity to pursue pet issues and as a rule, the further they go from home to serve, the less likely they are to address campaign issues. A city council member who campaigned that he intended to hold the line on taxes has a greater opportunity of exerting this sort of influence than does a U.S. representative, who will seldom see a bill that clearly raises or lowers taxes.

As a result, most political analysts regard this type of issue at a maximum of 15 percent of the total bills a legislator will vote on. About the only way of increasing this percentage is to keep careful records of what a legislator said as a candidate and then be creative about pointing out how a current bill applies to those promises.

Adding the moral issues to the campaign promises we still have 80 percent of the issues to account for. This last 80 percent is the area in which lobbyists try to operate and in which legislators at all levels really can be influenced.

This large, final group of issues relates back to a legislator's personal experience. When evaluating his trust or mistrust of a given piece of legislation, a legislator will quickly run through the moral issue and campaign issue category. Next he will stop to ponder a bit based on past occupation, acquaintances, family member occupations, jobs done when a child, place of upbringing and other basic background influences. The strongest of these are determined by the region where he grew up, parents' background, and commonly held views of constituents.

For all practical matters this is the only area in which a legislator can be influenced. It may take a well-thought-through strategy that recognizes the person's roots and beliefs, but it can be done in this area and probably not the others.

The trick for the lobbyist is to know the legislator's background so well that material relating to the bill can be presented to the legislator in a manner that it stimulates past experiences in the desired fashion. A legislator who grew up on a farm is going to pay more attention to farm bills. One whose dad had a machine shop that sold parts to Lockheed will feel he knows quite a bit about workers' compensation, small business financing, sales to the military, and so on.

The task for the Political Action Group in this case is not easy. It must gather reams of background material. Put yourself in the legislator's place. If at all possible, find a person in the group who has had a similar occupation or upbringing and ask him to relate to the bill or rule. Knowing what one is aiming for makes the task more plausible. Stretch your ingenuity to frame the presentation for the legislator's roots and interests.

Analyzing the Electorate

Unfortunately, explaining why citizens vote as they do cannot be reduced to quite as simple a formula. But two philosophical ground rules are the core of any analysis of why citizens vote as they do. They are related, but not by means that are immediately obvious. Generally people tend to vote in this pattern for both issues and candidates.

Rule 1: Citizens will vote either for the status quo if they know what that is or, in the case of multiple candidates, for the one they dislike the least.

Rule 2: People cannot help but react to cross pressures. The cross-pressure theory of voting patterns suggests that the majority of voters will follow their historic trend.

Although analysts have known for years about the effect of cross pressures on ballot initiatives, they are just beginning to realize how they apply to elected candidates. Those who have been Republicans, Democrats, liberals or conservatives, will continue to vote that pattern. Those who, for instance, have traditionally voted no on school bonds will tend to continue to vote no.

The theory in more detail says that voters will be exposed to pressures to change their position. These may be new arguments or slogans or new information—anything that works against the status quo. The theory is that, given these voters' predisposition to vote as they traditionally have, they will—before voting again—look for some sort of reinforcement for their position. In addition, they will attempt to block out and ignore any information that has a tendency to persuade them to vote against their historic position. This is a tendency your PAG can put to use.

If the voter is successful in maintaining his intellectual isolation, by blocking and/or rationalizing the contradictory information he is receiving, he will relieve the pressure to vote in a manner that is basically unpalatable to him. Therefore, if the PAG wants voters to maintain their usual pattern, it will do all it can to screen out the cross pressures and reinforce the voters' basic thinking. Voters, freed of their doubts, will go to the polls and happily vote in the predisposed manner.

In the opposite case, if the voter is subjected to a comprehensive, persuasively presented program that he cannot rationalize away, the cross pressures will build and cause voter discomfort. The result is, some voters will find some excuse not to vote on election day.

The strategy in this case is to provide one's followers with strong, strident, one-sided reasons for going along with the group on the issue at hand. The arguments may by nature be extremely tough and one-sided (which is another reason for keeping amateur philosophers and recreational debaters out of the campaign). We do not want objectively to look at both sides of the issue. The firm—yet appropriate—message will reinforce those predisposed to vote with the group while casting doubt in the minds of those who had intended to vote in opposition. In applying this technique to candidates, the aim is to move the undecideds to vote with the group and so demoralize the opposition voters that they stay home.

Careful polling, aided by the best thought of your brain trust, should bring out the negatives for both initiatives and/or candidates. Knowing the negatives, the PAG can bring serious cross pressures to bear. This is exactly how the Left uses health-related environmental issues in referenda to bamboozle well-intentioned people to give up their factories, jobs and reasonably priced power, among other things.

Readers who have never pondered this syndrome will now see the place of charge and counter-charge in a campaign. Candidates using their latest polling data are trying to give people reasons either to stay home or to stay with them.

On a year-in, year-out basis, the syndrome still works best on locally contested, bond levies, school board overrides, initiative measures and such-like. It will work on legislative contests, but as one moves further up the national political scale, it does not work quite as well. It does not easily succeed because presidents, U.S. senators and representatives all hire very able pollsters and political consultants who keep all of this sorted out. The contest becomes, at worst, one of your popgun against their air force. A huge amount of mud is thrown, usually with minimal observable impact.

The group with the most ammunition will persuade you not to vote for their candidate, but to vote against the other guy. This theory also leads to the truth that people seldom vote for somebody they like. Most voters cast their ballots against the candidate they like the least. As it works out they are voting against something rather than for a person or issue. Sadly, this is the heart and soul of modern American politics. And since we, as a society and as participants in the political process, have discovered that it is much easier to convince a voter to oppose than to support, it is likely that the attack principle will remain central to American politics for the foreseeable future.

On the local level, speakers bureaus, direct mail brochures, media ads, news stories and other tactics apply cross pressures leading to the defeat of repressive school boards, state senators and, at times, a national figure or two. These theories are devastating when integrated into a coherent strategy.

Chapter 15

Fact Sheet

I f the PAG is to make any lobbying effort, such as appearing at a rally inside the state capitol, it is essential that the rank and file be thoroughly briefed. An important starting point for such instruction is the preparation of a group fact sheet.

Getting out a fact sheet for one's foot soldiers is simple—but be sure it's done! Many groups overlook this easy device and regret it later.

The most immediately important aspect of a fact sheet is merely to let the PAG foot soldiers know that something is being done. Fact sheets brief the group on the objective and plan for action. So long as the leadership is clear in its own thinking, the writing, editing, typing and printing can often be finished in a matter of hours. This gives both opponents and supporters the impression that the group is off to an auspicious start and knows what it's doing.

Time permitting, the contents of the fact sheet should be thoroughly discussed by the brain trust. All facts, figures and data pertinent to the campaign at that time should be included in concise, summary form. This so everyone is quoting the same figures. Research all of the information methodically and meticulously. Even if some of the material is not used, file it away till the campaign is over. Keep all supporting documents in the same file. Just be sure no pertinent data are dropped out. In the case of complex facts and figures, work hard at condensing them and clarify them as much as possible. Keep in mind the poor souls who are trying to sell their neighbors on the idea of voting with the group. If they can't keep track of all the complications, they will be ineffective and may be embarrassed. Keep it simple.

Tiny groups, having money for nothing else, can almost always get out a fact sheet. It may be, and often is, cheap; but the sheet should never look cheap. It may be the first tangible effort of the group, yet might also be on the shelves longer than most other materials. Print the sheet on high-quality paper. Use cover stock, anticipating that the sheet will sometimes be used as a poster. The best fact sheets, in our opinion, are those that place all of the data on one side of one sheet of quality paper. If necessary, use two sides of the same sheet but carefully set out an outline of the main facts, using boldface type, Roman numerals or whatever else. Make the sheet or sheets easy to read.

Fact sheets are not copies of news releases. The writing style is factual; it is not a newspaper editorial. Write the sheet in such a way that difficult-to-remember facts and figures are presented as part of a permanent record, not as an unfolding story complete with background material. Time and circumstances permitting, it is helpful to run a poll before writing the fact sheet. A poll will allow the brain trust to consider the major issues of the campaign, folding them into the sheet that will, as a result, have a much greater impact.

Always include a one- or two-sentence conclusion that calls for action. Keep in mind that on the level of a campaign, this is no longer a philosophical debate. Marching orders and conclusions should come through loud and clear without respect for other possible sides of the issue.

The marginal cost for printing additional thousands of fact sheets is always very low. Photocopying is much more expensive than printing for the volumes of fact sheets you should use. It doesn't take much bravery to produce significant numbers so that everyone in the group can have many.

At the end of a hotly contested campaign, you may look around for just one more small batch of brochures to plug a small hole in your door-to-door distribution program, to place in a literature rack or to use as posters—only to find the only material remaining is a couple of reams of original fact sheets you completely forgot about. Press them into service. Invariably they work wonderfully. At this late point in the campaign it often doesn't matter so much what the material says as that the voters find a piece of literature on their doorstep yet again.

Don't forget: As part of an effective initiative campaign, the group should locate every reporter's home in the city and be sure that all receive a piece of literature on the doorstep at least once every two weeks. Also distribute the same pamphlet to a reporter's immediate neighbors, since they may mention it to him. The effect is psychological. Reporters assume every home in the area was blanketed by the group's literature distribution team. They will also assume a very disciplined, well organized group is at work on the issue. That newspaper will be reluctant to write off or ignore this kind of a group.

Chapter 16

Videos

B oth the Democrats and the Republicans run six- to ten-day candidate training schools. They charge a princely sum for new candidates and their campaign managers who come to party headquarters to learn the art of getting elected. The schools are highly regarded by most participants as being the place where the latest state of the art campaign strategy, calendar management, office management, fund raising, effective media relations and many other related items can be learned.

Probably the most important skill among the priorities of both parties is TV appearance. After only a brief acclimation period the candidate is pushed in front of a video camera where professional analysts mercilessly critique his or her dress, demeanor and general performance. It is often a humiliating experience for otherwise arrogant, self-assured candidate types.

Most average, hard-working freedom advocates do not realize the power TV has over our society. Independent-minded people, the self-employed and nearly all successful business people tend to watch TV only briefly, perhaps mainly for the news. They do not appreciate what can be done with TV, nor do they know what it costs or how to be effective with that medium.

The president of a huge corporation who agreed to ramrod a political project said in all seriousness to forget everything else: all the money would be spent producing and running TV commercials. "By the time we are done they won't get three votes," he said. His plan may have worked. However, he never got the chance to try. The brain trust finally persuaded the crusty old warhorse to accept a balanced campaign, albeit one that included a big shot of TV.

On the other side, a freedom fighter who has stood with us on many tough issues maintains that for every hour one watches TV, a one-point drop in IQ occurs. He may be right as well. It is tough to get this fellow to spend any money at all on TV.

For better or for worse, TV is a fact of life for political activists. We must deal with two related and often complementary uses of video. These are (1) professional TV commercials for use in the group's media and (2) building a documentary library for use against the bureaucracy during a campaign.

In this day of cheap and increasingly cheaper video equipment there is no reason for a serious Political Action Group not to use video technology. Video gear can be either purchased or rented for a modest sum. It is vital for evidence-gathering, presentations and training.

Video cameras are absolutely priceless for capturing one-time events on film that can be used later as a propaganda device. Getting some footage of the police roughly hauling the parents of a private-school student off to jail, the kids coming home to an empty house, the horrible wounds suffered by workers as a result of enviro-sabotage activity, businesses being shut down by the tax collectors, and on and on, are very effective after the campaign gets rolling.

Once the event is on film the group can grind out dozens of copies to be distributed to local, regional and even national TV. If the camera is rolling during the entire imbroglio and the quality of the material is fairly high, including capture of some especially flagrant events, the media are quite likely to rerun a thirty- to forty-second segment every time the group has a news conference or otherwise attracts media attention.

Purchase vs. rental is a decision that must be made early in the campaign at the time the strategy is written. Groups that intend to catch the bureaucracy acting like tyrants or expect the media to try to trap them find that having a video camera close at hand is good insurance. If all the events of the campaign are predictable, rental on the days of need should be adequate.

Video equipment has many uses during the campaign that novices might not anticipate. These range from training speakers to producing video slide shows to recording one-time events for eventual use as news clips. The one major use to which political groups should not put their video equipment is making their own

TV commercials. TV commercials are very difficult to produce correctly, so this is a job for professionals.

Another excellent and often overlooked use of a video camera is to minimize the arbitrary impact of people with police powers who are hostile toward the group. Bureaucrats suddenly become very subdued when a group member shows up carrying a video camera. They detest being captured on film even if they are 100 percent certain the law is on their side.

Bureaucrats tend to sing a wholly different tune as long as the camera is around. Be liberal with film and batteries and be pushy so that every move an overstepping government official makes is recorded for all of history. The cost is trivial compared to the power of your footage.

Harassed, unfairly treated businessmen, for instance, using their own film crews, stopped the high-handed abuses of the people from "20/20" and "60 Minutes" dead in their tracks. The latter can no longer engage in ambush interviews. Businessmen have learned to say "make an appointment at my office or I will come to your office. I will also bring my own film crew with me." The technique has stopped muckraking reporters from dishonestly taking one small, isolated statement made by a citizen they detest and molding it into something with an entirely different meaning.

Tape recorders have a similar impact when placed in front of hostile print media people. Use a tape recorder, if necessary, but try to develop rapport with the person so that recording is not necessary. A group's recorder mixed with the others in a pile at a news conference is psychologically neutral. One set out alone at a meeting with a newsman could be offensive. However, the situation may be past any concerns about offending. Each situation must be evaluated individually.

Set your own camera up at news conferences. This is to have a complete record of the proceedings for the PAG file. TV media people are seldom dishonestly hostile, requiring a documentary video, when other news people are also present.

Unless the group spokesman is skilled and experienced, he or she should spend all the hours it takes—and learning can take many hours, days, weeks—in front of the TV camera, rehearsing answers to likely questions as proposed by the brain trust.

Should the group decide to debate, expect to spend hours with the group spokesman in front of the camera perfecting the pitch. Nothing should be left undone. No question unanswered. The demands on the staff under these circumstances are such that they alone make a good case against agreeing to debate.

If at all possible, use the standard ¾-inch commercial video-tape format. This equipment is big, cumbersome, and expensive. A few amateurs have this equipment and many companies in larger cities rent them to professional filming crews among others. Under no circumstances short of absolute crisis use the miniature 8-mm photographic film format. Most really potent videos will be done as news feeds of one-time events. Unless it is something truly remarkable such as the EPA shooting a farmer for spraying his fields, or the sighting of a Sasquatch, the TV stations will not use the inferior formats.

VHS format, which is ½-inch, is commonly available to purchase and to rent. The TV stations will grumble about having to reformat to ¾-inch but usually they will take VHS tapes and use them.

By the time you need this manual, technical advances may have hit the market. The rage as of this writing in high-tech circles is the high-resolution ½-inch Professional Beta format that even network news teams use. If you have access and funding, buy one. The news gatherers and their studios are being converted because of resolution, clarity, light weight and low cost. You should have the same advantages.

Chapter 17

Slide Shows

S lide shows that portray the group's position, agenda and goals are a superb method of carrying the battle into the enemy's territory. Words can go in one ear and out the other, but pictures stick and give your message impact. This technique can be used to magnify your effectiveness on almost any political issue.

Slide shows gather additional impact from the fact that an otherwise inarticulate, shy person can run the slides for a friend or group of friends. Once the series is put together, marginal costs to run the show yet again, even for a single individual, are modest.

Probably the biggest single advantage of a well-planned slide show is that it will cover all the bases. Amateur presenters need not fear that they will forget a key element, argument or statistic vital to the campaign. All of the important information can be conveyed. Knowing the content, the presenter can be ready to take the viewers' questions (there are bound to be some) afterward regarding the issues covered. Skilled, seasoned presenters learn to back the show up while saying "in response to your questions we have found the following . . ." as the appropriate slides are rerun.

Revising the script or adding new, more up-to-date slides, is easy with a slide show. Movies and videos, in contrast, are difficult to revise, and thus are not nearly as versatile. Supposing that polling conducted during the campaign suggests that critical elements have been neglected or are no longer an issue, it is relatively easy to revamp the slide series appropriately.

One downside to scripted slide presentations is that the production takes some skill and, almost always, a lot of time. The script commonly takes twenty to fifty hours to write. You will need a competent, dedicated individual with the time to put it together. Doing a professional-looking slide show with script, photos and synchronization is almost more than inexperienced freedom fighters can be expected to accomplish in-house for the group. Any experienced or professional sources you can draw on for assistance are a big help.

Equipment needed to run slide shows is expensive to very expensive. Projector and synchronizing tape players can be rented or borrowed but require semi-skilled volunteers to set up and run. If the group has access to a video camera, a computer and a recorder, the job can be made somewhat simpler and cheaper. It is possible to videotape slide shows without synchronizing unit or dual projectors. Simply set the camera up and run a tape of your announcer reading the script. Be sure to use a skilled, authoritative-sounding announcer (if all else fails, hire a DJ from the local radio station). As you play your video, run the slides through the projectors manually.

Of course, the process described is now considered paleolithic, for any school kid handy with a computer and graphics software can turn out a "professional" presentation. But the result is still acceptable and much simpler and easier to run than projectors and tape synchronizers. Videos of slide shows are cheap and easy to duplicate, assuming the demand for the show increases as expected. Video players are widely used, so in most instances, the needed equipment will already be in place and ready to go. The video method is ideal for small gatherings but not the best when the group is larger than about twenty-five.

Make two versions of the slide show. The first should last sixteen minutes. This is to be used at service club luncheons. It may be difficult to incorporate all the key arguments, facts and figures in this shorter program, but give it your best shot. When it seems appropriate, have a twenty-five-minute version containing more strident material. Both programs are to be heavily laced with propaganda, but the longer production should definitely be more hard core. Use the long one among the core group, as a group recruitment tool and as the principal tool for showing on TV.

The general public will usually turn out to see a well-done, dramatic presentation. This is more true when the group has done its ancillary homework regarding news conferences, paid media, direct mail regional organization and fund raising. But keep in mind that even interested, dedicated supporters will seldom sit through the showing more than once. Most people are members of several groups. As the speakers bureau does its work and the show makes its final rounds, attendance may be expected to lag.

Writing slide show scripts is done by formula. Slides can be taken by semi-professionals or even by competent amateurs. When the script is written, list your needs and have your photographer get the best, most dramatic slides needed for each situation. Not all the shots will be available but the list does provide an ideal goal for those putting the slide show together.

A computer is used to construct necessary charts, graphs and captions used in the slide show. You can easily have a so-called Post-Script® service bureau print graphs, charts or slides directly from computer files. Political activists in remote areas or small towns should look at the literature included with presentation software for computers which advertises mail-in services. Just mail the disk with your graph saved to it, and in a few days the postman delivers your professional presentation graphics.

The biggest failings of novice slide shows are (1) not running slides through fast enough and (2) not featuring enough slides of people doing things that make the group's point. Audiences like to see people doing things but limit viewing to three or four seconds per slide. Move right along.

The following in brief, truncated form is the formula most often used by slide show scriptwriters.

1. The first element of an effective script should consist of a common point of identification on which virtually every viewer can agree. Example: Traditionally residents of River City have enjoyed an enjoyable, unique standard of living and quality of life.
   A. Aerial shot of city.
   B. People at picnic.
   C. Boat in driveway with people loading for use.
2. Next put in a bridge. Example: We have maintained this standard by being a caring, concerned community where we knew and cared about each other.
   A. Shot of people on busy street.
   B. Citizen helping police at scene of accident.
   C. Young girl carrying grocery bag for her grandmother.

3. Start polarizing the viewers by use of buzz words that will get the viewers' blood flowing. Example: In a growing, prospering, vital community such as River City, our children have traditionally not been forced to leave the area to find employment. Our tax base grew with the community. As we grew and prospered, the services we were able to offer grew as well. Everyone pulled his own weight.
   A. 1900s era slide of Main Street.
   B. Various shots of city maps starting in 1930 to present.
   C. Bar graph showing expenditures for human programs.
   D. Shots of business under construction.

4. Throw in some facts and figures that look authoritative in nature and that build credibility. Example: In 1970 our assessed valuation was $190 million. A total of 483 people were employed in the River City area. By 1985 approximately 28 businesses had closed their doors but, because of the opportunity and vision of our residents, a total of 283 new businesses were started for a net gain of 255. River City's assessed valuation increased almost threefold to over $500 million. Our city had budgets running over $4 million to spend on new streets, sewers and water, fire and police protection.
   A. Bar graph of assessed valuation.
   B. Workers coming out of factory.
   C. People in shopping center.
   D. Bar graph showing growth in city revenue.
   E. Fire station.
   F. New street or sewer being put in place.
   G. New prosperous homes.

5. Introduce the villain and start the attack. Example: Our city has never run its accounts in the red. Traditionally budgets were balanced while the needs of our citizens were always adequately met. Now we are faced with a negative city council which, while denying the right of our children to live and work with us in River City, also has the audacity to ask us to increase our taxes so as to cover its foolish spending, which has left the finances of the city in disarray.
   A. Shot of little kids in school.
   B. Bar graph dramatically displaying spending increases.
   C. Bar graph showing city borrowing.

D. Pie chart showing city expenditures for RV stations, bicycle paths, travel to out of state conventions.

E. People at city council meeting.

6. Continue the attack. Example: Collectively council members have driven away or discouraged new businesses bringing new job-creating ideas. On the flimsiest of personal reasons they have refused to allow for adequate zoning of land needed for new business, including stores and shops that will conveniently supply the needs of residents who do not want to drive ninety miles to another market area.

A. Shot of store boarded up.

B. Aerial photo showing limited available commercial land outlined in red.

C. Long, open road to adjoining community.

D. Youngsters with suitcases departing the city.

7. Blame the guilty. Example: Our very own elected representatives have discouraged our entrepreneurs to the point that many have left town.

A. Graph showing sharp decline in building.

B. City council sitting looking Scrooge-like.

C. People walking by a "no help wanted" sign in store.

8. Others also blame the guilty. Example: Businessmen with big dollars to spend have come to River City with the intent of building job-producing taxpaying factories.

A. Written statement from a well-known local resident condemning the city zoning policy.

B. Bar graph showing newspaper ad revenues and pages published trending down.

C. Title showing cost of running planning and zoning office.

D. Police and fire department budgets shown declining in relative terms.

E. Bar graph showing personal tax/income sacrificed.

9. Call for action. Example: But on November 3 you have two big chances to bring River City back to its traditional values. To allow the city to grow and prosper and to call to task the reckless members of our elected government who have allowed the city's finances to fall into such a sorry state of disrepair. "Vote Yes on the Levy Override Containment Initiative." The second measure would remove authority for land-use decision mak-

ing from the nameless, faceless bureaucrats at the planning and zoning commission and return it to the hands of the people. "Vote Yes on Measure X as well."

A.   People voting and polling place.

B.   Bar graph showing total assessment going up. Arrow breaking through initiative barrier.

C.   Beautiful residential district.

D.   Black box dramatizing city debt.

E.   Pictures of citizens saying "I am voting Yes" with initiative wording set out in entirety.

F.   Picture of citizen saying "I am going to decide what's best for River City because this is my home."

10. Describe in detail the action needed. Example: You can "Vote Yes" to both measures November 3 and help get River City back on a solid path toward its traditional values.

A.   Projected growth in construction.

B.   Slide showing projected growth in employment.

C.   Slide showing projected growth in value of construction.

D.   Happy workers coming out of factory.

E.   Additional letter of endorsement for concept from noted citizen.

F.   Title slide showing date and exact ballot wording.

This is a simple example. But even very complex, many-faceted issues can be handled in a similar fashion using the same formula. The more complex, the more the issues must be dissected and looked at a piece at a time.

When possible, make heavy use of testimonials and newspaper statements that endorse your cause. These spread a web of credibility over the entire project. If other organizations have endorsed the group's goals, list these endorsements along with a brief shot of the group doing the endorsing and its endorsing statement.

Your slide show is a tool to be used at every opportunity. Audience reaction will help you refine it, if needed. It should be among the first devices to try when setting up a PAG, especially if there is a problem with public opinion. It will keep serving until the job is done.

Chapter 18

Speakers Bureau

A speaker, representing your group before other organizations in the community, obviously can help you gain support and financing. But why just one? Two, five, *lots* of speakers can multiply your support tremendously.

Properly trained and equipped, your speakers can get to hundreds of places and talk to thousands of people on behalf of the group. They can, given proper organizational support, create a wave of information so fast and reaching so far that the opposition can never recover. Once the group has an active speakers program in place, operating unchecked by the opposition, there is little that can overcome the group's lead. The best way to do this is to set up a speakers bureau for the group.

Speakers bureaus maximize the ability of gifted speakers and at the same time can employ relatively inarticulate members of the rank and file to win the hearts and minds of the people.

There are five key steps necessary for organizing an effective speakers bureau. These are:

1. Developing a packaged presentation.
2. Identifying and training group speakers.
3. Securing speaking engagements.
4. Scheduling.
5. Maintaining central coordination.

Scheduling is the crucial function. If you can afford only one paid position, it should be the person who keeps the scheduling book, takes and makes reservations, and then follows up to be sure that the group's aspiring orators actually get to their events, in good condition to do their work.

The group should develop a presentation that its speakers can rely on heavily. This should include analysis of the issues by the brain trust, perhaps published as a fact sheet; a slide show if at all possible; and a few stock easy-to-deliver speeches. Brochures produced as part of a door-to-door or direct mail campaign can be integrated into the presentation if available, and passed out at meetings.

Should the group have nothing more than a basic fact sheet and a slide show, consider this as an excellent basis with which to organize a speakers bureau. Don't wait for the other side to organize. Keep the group's momentum going by sending out the speakers. Once the Other Side realizes that we have people out addressing groups, their reaction will constitute one of the real enjoyments of this business.

Having all these materials nicely organized makes the job of finding speakers relatively easy. Let's call them "presenters," in case people are nervous about public speaking. And presenting the group's positions and goals is the whole point, not delivering an oration. Almost anyone can do it. Average presenters who are otherwise reluctant to take controversial material out before the public will usually do so readily, knowing that they have a ready-made, battle-tested package. That should make recruitment easy.

Start by having members of the Political Action Group, in conjunction with the brain trust and group spokesman, make an exhaustive list of potential speakers bureau members. As soon as you have this list, you can start recruiting. The more presenters you have, the better. In many cases the opportunities to present are limited only by the number of presenters. Your members (many of whom are potential presenters) belong to other groups, all of which are potential targets.

Before taking the show on the road, group presenters should take ample time to study the material and to practice. Seasoned members can coach and encourage new presenters at practices. When the presenters begin to address other groups, key members of the Political Action Group should go along for encouragement, and to be available after the show to answer questions. Schedule sufficient time so that all questions and concerns can be discussed freely and candidly. Presenters who feel there are holes in the group's logic or who feel that background research was inadequate will not prove to be enthusiastic concerning the cause. Be sure this is ironed out in advance.

Training the new presenters will require a basic short course on equipment use, assembly, operation and debugging. This can be a bit daunting. We have had volunteers "unvolunteer" when they saw the maze of wire boxes and lenses scattered out in disarray on the counter! At times you may well have to assign a separate technician to handle special gear. Videos are simpler but do not lend themselves well to audiences of more than twenty to thirty people.

Scheduling

Assigning speaking engagements is hugely more time-consuming than the novice political activist would ever suppose. Lists of clubs, groups and associations in even modest-sized communities, obtained from the chamber of commerce or local political offices, can run four or five pages. When church circles, hunting clubs, model airplane clubs and other such are included, the list can become truly formidable.

It is cumbersome and far from ideal for the campaign staff to call all these organizations with the suggestion that next time they need a program, the group will be happy to send over a qualified speaker and slide show. Contacting and scheduling soon consume too much staff time. Other crises may arise, pushing the vital speakers bureau function to the back burner.

To overcome this problem, identify three or four volunteers who like to talk on the phone, are committed to the campaign ideals and are willing to put in the time to help. They can use the service club list compiled by the campaign staff, calling each president or secretary with an offer to have your presenter appear before that group. As soon as an invitation is accepted and a program arranged, the contact person should call group headquarters with the information.

Staffers at headquarters will then take the engagement date and match it to a speaker from the speakers bureau list. In the case of a group known to be difficult, the staff may want to pick a person of superior ability.

After confirming the speaker's availability on that date, the staffer should fill out and distribute a speakers bureau form like this one, so that everyone is clear about assignments:

Speakers Bureau Assignment

Date _____

Name of Club _____

Contact Person _____

Phone _____

Contact Person's Title _____

Date of Scheduled Presentation _____

Time and Place of Presentation _____

_____

Speaker Taking Assignment _____

Person Who Made Contact _____

Equipment Needed _____

_____

Asking for Financial Support Approved?   ☐ Yes   ☐ No

Asking for Support Resolution Approved? ☐ Yes   ☐ No

Comments _____

_____

_____

Be sure everyone knows where the meeting is to be held and be especially at pains to ensure that necessary equipment will be available on the agreed-upon date.

Having tied down date, speaker, equipment and contact, enter the listing on a master calendar. Using a large monthly calendar set out in the office on an easel or the wall will garner extra support from visitors who can plainly see that the campaign is building. Send copies of the assignment sheets to the club president, the speaker, the equipment people, as necessary, always keeping one copy in the office.

In our experience, propagandizing and raising money are best handled separately. It is usually best if the slide show itself is subtle about asking for monetary support; the presenter can, if the speaker and the club officers so agree, ask for financial support from the target organization. Our Side is traditionally a bit bashful about asking for money for political projects—perhaps too bashful.

If not money, ask for a club resolution supporting the group's position. It is helpful if the presenter has a stock resolution to pass out containing the proper "Whereases" and the requisite "Be it resolveds," etc. Then the target group can, in the first flush of conversion, pass the necessary resolution.

Even if the club does not endorse your group's position, the presentation may cause it to remain officially neutral, thus denying its official support to the opposition. Many times this is a great victory by itself.

Like so many elements of a political action campaign, forming a speakers bureau is not difficult. It takes some time and skill to organize but is wonderfully effective once put in motion. The difficult part is putting the fact sheet and slide show together, so it is important to tackle these early.

Chapter 19

Strange Bedfellows Welcome!

In politics, numbers are the name of the game, and coalitions are one of the quickest, most effective ways to multiply your numbers. Don't worry that politics creates strange—at times extremely strange—bedfellows. Rarely is another group so tainted that we can't accept its support for *our* objective. The fledgling PAG should learn not only to take whatever support might be out there but also to be creative and persuasive about going after it.

Multitudes of groups exist that can, if the proper handle is found, be encouraged to support groups of free-market advocates. Service clubs, chambers of commerce, unions, churches, youth groups, hunting clubs, service clubs, temperance unions, political organizations, environmental groups and dozens more like these should all be viewed as potential supporters until they positively indicate otherwise. Nursing boards, arts and crafts groups, model airplane clubs, farmers' organizations, canoe clubs, hikers' associations, archery clubs, medical associations, antique collectors, retired citizens, and library boards are among the many that have been enlisted through the years.

An often overlooked source of support is with the bureaucracy itself. Clever political manipulators will attempt to get county commissioners' support against the city, city attorneys against the city council, the sheriff against the police, economic development officer against the county commissioner, the fire department against the city, and so on. Look through the governmental offices section of the phone book. Be inquisitive, identifying any office possible that might oppose the Enemy of the Day. Then go to it with your proposal and best sales pitch.

Whenever an organization with major regional clout comes on line, consider involving it in a joint news conference. Usually these groups are delighted for the chance for some publicity that someone else professionally organizes. Draw up for these people a news release that incorporates as much of your material as you can reasonably get away with.

Your challenge is to get a handle on the associations and then to think up the one good reason that they should join your parade. In many instances, these groups have never been pitched by anyone with a freedom agenda containing exhortation to overt, constructive political action. Some, you will find, do not know how to act or to react. Even so, some members may become constituents of the concept even though the group itself does not immediately sign on. If the group makes a weak or seemingly dubious statement supporting your PAG, that still shuts the door to the Other Side and adds numbers to yours.

Coalitions, by themselves, won't win elections. They should, however, constantly be in the back of political activists' minds as the momentum builds. The more desperate your cause, the more your PAG needs to seek support in every quarter. Keep an open mind, and others will open theirs.

Chapter 20

Letters

L etters to the editor and letters to one's congressman have a direct, dramatic impact on the political process. Both kinds of letter are easy for even a novice to write, delivering impact beyond what one might logically expect.

Letters to the editor use someone else's (often antagonistic) medium to build credibility for the group's objectives and goals. A handful of letters, timed well, can create the impression that a PAG or an idea enjoys a large body of support among the readership of the publication. They can also stir up controversy, convey information, subtly ask for contributions and, at times, be used to keep issues alive during otherwise flat spots in a campaign.

Letters on issues are usually more effective than those written in support of specific candidates. In either case, readers will seldom read letters longer than three paragraphs with three sentences to the paragraph. They tend to scan the title inserted by the newspaper staff, the reader's name and then, if their curiosity is aroused, the body of the letter. Therefore, when you write, go straight to your point, as persuasively and in as few words as possible.

Be a good spokesman: the *tone* of your letter exemplifies the idea you are selling. Even a letter expressing outrage should be stated in a magnanimous spirit. If you are rude or sullen or mean, you'll tar your own project. Avoid anything that hints of personal attack, bad manners or obscenity. Never fabricate a letter to the editor. Papers often phone to verify name and address.

Most regional and local papers will run almost any courteous, to-the-point and passably written letter they receive from readers.

Large papers get too many letters to run them all but are still worth a try. In fact, give them your best effort because they have the best impact when you succeed in getting a letter published. Papers editorially hostile to the group's position often have a liberal letter publishing policy that can be turned to Our Side's advantage.

Occasionally editors will shorten or abridge the material readers send them, when the writer is verbose or tries to cover too many points at one sitting. It is an annoying chore for them when they must do it. Be sure *your* letter is concise and not in need of editing. The editors will appreciate it and your chances for being published are far better. Don't worry about their changing the meaning of your letter (unethical for them and just not done) or shrinking from controversial or hostile points of view. Quite the contrary, newspapers love controversy—it sells more papers—and enjoy publishing hostile letters to stir up their own troops.

Voters generally look for reinforcement for their predisposed position but do react to seemingly large numbers of letters from credible writers with the opposite view. A careful letter-writing campaign may cause some voters either to change their minds or to move into the undecided column. Letters calling over and over again for answers to fair-sounding questions make the Other Side look as if it is covering something up, and so have dramatic impact.

Planning a Letter Campaign

Organizing a letter-writing campaign may seem to the novice freedom fighter to be a walk in the park. In fact, it is not easy at all. Most people do not enjoy writing political letters and, as a result, write poorly. When they finally do agree to participate, they procrastinate in the most maddening fashion. Keep nagging in a friendly way. Set up a letter to the editor file and show the great results to the group—as a message to procrastinators. If possible, go outside your PAG as well. You can keep the media and the opposition off balance by using endorsements from unsuspected places. Getting a local airline office to send a letter on its letterhead in support of home schools, for instance, really catches people off guard.

If the campaign ultimately delivers half the letters planned, it is an outstanding success. Most times you do not get 10 percent. The best letter senders usually are the rank-and-file, lower-level precinct workers. Worst are corporate types who never seem to be able to get around to having their secretary retype our form letter on their letterhead for signature.

A perfect campaign would consist of writing perhaps a dozen letters composed by the professional staff, distributed to key members of the Political Action Group in the area. Ideally these letters would end up in the editor's office, retyped on members' stationery, during the first few weeks of the campaign. After that, request that your group send letters, and a few independent communications may turn up in the editor's office from time to time. Toward the end of the campaign, compose another batch, in the office, for distribution to your people.

These last letters should be structured to ask questions and name names—especially those of pesty bureaucrats—of those whom campaign experience has shown to be particularly sensitive to criticism. Bureaucrats loathe having their names turn up in the daily paper. It is alien to their nature to accommodate such a turn of events. If it happens two or three times, it may be more than they can handle. Freedom fighters can further polarize the situation by sending clippings without comment to the bureaucrat's supervisor at the next level up. After this happens a time or two, the clippings will end up in the bureaucrat's employment file, creating problems for years on end.

A second, often overlooked device is to visit with the editor about doing a guest editorial. Unless the author is notoriously a literary klutz, the request is often granted, especially by smaller papers. Editors look kindly on this device as a means of both massaging their need to appear to be somewhat fair and building readership by creating controversy.

Rules for letters to the editor are uncomplicated:

1. Use plain white, high-quality paper unless you have your own good letterhead.
2. Use simple, declarative sentences (subject, verb, object). Long, complicated sentences will lose readers or be a "turn-off" to them.

3. Try to make two or three points at most. Do not allow the letter to exceed three paragraphs containing three sentences per paragraph.
4. Be certain the letter contains a daytime telephone number where the writer can be contacted. Most papers call and verify the author/sender.
5. *Spelling and grammar must be letter perfect.* Papers opposed to the writer's point of view will use—and with "(sic)" subtly call attention to—spelling and grammar imperfections to discredit the concept the writer espouses.
6. Use humor whenever possible. Our Side needs more of this.

Letters to Your Congressmen

Use a similar, direct, courteous approach in letters to your state or congressional representatives. The names and addresses can be obtained from newspapers, libraries, the League of Women Voters, the chamber of commerce or a politician's regional office. Send letters to congressmen to:

- Comment about pending legislation.
- Point out inequities in current law.
- Ask how the legislator intends to vote on a particular bill.
- Question or support that legislator's stand on an issue.
- Ask for help in forcing a bureaucrat to do his job and only his job, or in otherwise dealing with the bureaucracy.
- Ask for clarification on an issue.
- Tell the legislator exactly what you feel should be done and, in some isolated cases, suggest a strategy by which that course of action might be taken.

These are the broad issue questions on which representatives and senators expect the most mail and are most likely to respond. Not every letter to a congressman will elicit the desired response, but every letter counts.

There are extra, simple rules for writing congressmen (beyond those listed above). They are few but must be followed:

1. Spell the name correctly and get the title right. Senators detest being called representatives and representatives senators, etc.

2. Keep the letter brief, never more than a page. Charts, graphs and news clippings can be attached or provided later if the legislator asks for them.
3. Letters must be clear and neat. A handwritten letter, if neat, is as good as or better than one typed.
4. When referring to current bills or troublesome regulations, refer to each by number. Be knowledgeable and be exact.
5. It is fine to send a letter asking for specific action, even if you are reasonably certain that legislator will not honor your request. At times the mass of public opinion will change his mind or your letter may lay the groundwork for future action.

There are a few absolute don'ts:

1. Do not *ever* use form letters circulated by Political Action Groups, under penalty of having this book blow up in your face.
2. For similar reasons, never parrot slogans or repeat items from group newsletters.
3. Never threaten or be personally nasty.
4. Don't stand on membership in Political Action Groups. Legislators are concerned about individual voters.
5. Do not apologize for writing. Congressmen are supposed to work for all of us.
6. Do not lie, exaggerate or overstate your case. Writers may get away with it once but, from then on, it's the circular file for letters from those who have betrayed the trust of legislators.
7. Don't brag about any ability or influence you may have.
8. Say nothing disparagingly about the congressman's staff. On the contrary, go out of your way to compliment the staff. Guess who usually sees the letter first and decides if the congressman will see it? Enough said.
9. Never send carbons or photocopies. Hard to imagine but these are even worse than form letters.
10. Don't become a pen pal with only one song to sing. Vary the letters, including a bit of humor or even news from home.

We must sheepishly admit that the number 1 don't was violated flagrantly and successfully by the American banking industry a few years ago. When the IRS threatened to impose withholding tax on savings accounts, banks enclosed a form letter to congressmen in customers' bank statements, and hundreds of thousands of letters piled up in legislators' offices. But the exception only proves the rule: If you can't *fill* the congressman's office with form letters, get him a nice, small box of sincere personal missives.

The letter-writing criteria listed above can also be used to communicate with state representatives and senators if that is appropriate. Some state legislators, on hearing the pitch on the phone, may request a letter along with supporting documents anyway. The secretary of state in most states will have a list of legislators including addresses, phone numbers and, in some states, a bit of bio-data. Letters to local officials are usually sent to establish some sort of permanent record on the subject.

Newcomers to this business generally believe that most legislators simply throw out letters they receive or completely ignore them. Sometimes they do, to be sure, but this is misleading. They always have a response system and you can affect the response by the quality of your letter. Legislators tend to respond negatively only if they are convinced the issue will not cost them votes. Therefore, when composing the letter, try to recall how the legislator stood on that issue during the last campaign. If your issue is new (often so), consider the legislator's background, couching your arguments in terms appropriate to it.

When the issue is unusually controversial, the congressman will have his staff divide the mail into two stacks, thus tabulating the nays and the yeas. In extreme cases the mail may even be weighed rather than counted. Unless you are known to the legislator, the only way you have to cut through this and reach your target is by the lucidity and force of your letter. All your care in writing pays.

When a legislator becomes truly sympathetic to the cause of a freedom fighter, he or she can help in a number of ways. Letter writers can tactfully suggest a number of actions, including:

1. Forwarding their own letter over the legislator's signature to an offending agency, suggesting that it back off. (This isn't the most common occurrence, but it has been known to happen.)
2. Requesting that the legislator take an active part cosponsoring

a bill that would ameliorate the situation or, at least, scare off the bureaucrats.

3. Volunteering to come to Washington, D.C., or the state capital to tell your PAG's horror story related to the results of the law in its present form. Writers who can report gross atrocities perpetrated by arrogant bureaucrats will usually be of great interest to legislators.

4. Ask the legislator to use his or her influence to request or schedule hearings on an issue.

5. It is even possible to ask the legislator to write to other committee chairmen opposing specific legislation or bureaucratic interpretation. This does not come easily but it does not hurt to ask in most cases.

Letters, like ideas, have consequences. They have power. Use them freely and often, but coordinate and schedule the campaigns with care as part of your PAG's conscious strategy.

Chapter 21

Fund Raising Letters

D irect mail is the heartbeat of grassroots political action. It's cheap (relatively), fast (depending on your post office), and effective (as long as your expectations about success aren't unrealistic). So, before we tour the wonderful world of what some of your targets call junk mail, let's review the Ten Commandments of All Direct Mail.

1. The appeal must look personal.
2. The letter should allow the reader the opportunity of a range of choices of action.
3. The appeal must be emotional.
4. The mailing must include some device which requires a response, even if the reader doesn't send money.
5. Every letter must contain a return envelope with a printed address.
6. The appeal must be based on content, not rhetoric. It must be passionate about a real issue. Be clear, be specific, explain exactly why you need the money.
7. Tell people what you will do with their donations. Promise an action to match their contribution.
8. State the appeal several different ways in the letter.
9. Make the envelope stand out and invite the reader to open it.
10. Be certain you have a good list, the right list, or your effort and money are worse than wasted. The list is everything, and you must qualify and refine it by continual testing.

Raising money is the primary purpose of direct mail. There are many ways to collect the cash necessary for political actions, but many groups rely heavily on mail solicitation for one rock solid reason: it works. Otherwise your mailbox wouldn't be full of fund appeals.

Fund raising by mail is done entirely by formula, making it the easiest, most certain device to organize. Once the group has gathered together mailing lists, the costs to get out money raising letters are relatively modest. Experienced money raisers know that historically 4 to 6 percent of those receiving *an effective* solicitation will respond and that every item in the formula that is properly executed will add a half percent to the total. But if you don't do it right, you will pour the PAG's money down the sink and get nothing for it.

The process can be roughly divided into two phases: writing the letter, then producing, printing and mailing it.

The formula for writing the body of an effective fund raising letter runs as follows:

1. Open the letter by identifying a common enemy or problem that both writer and recipient can readily agree on. Openers that are strident and tough generally command the greatest attention, but the opener must be brief. (See examples at the end of this chapter.)
2. Establish a common bond that cements everyone together in opposition to the common enemy.
3. Next, in a paragraph or two, tell about the Political Action Group and how it will solve the commonly identified problem. (This section is often the most lengthy in the letter.)
4. Now is the time to ask for money for the first time in the letter. Ask for "help" in the first few sentences here, or the reader's mind will wander.
5. Tell exactly where the money will be spent. This crucial step is too often omitted by novices.
6. Enumerate to the readers how the candidate or the Political Action Group has already invested heavily in the campaign.
7. Set a deadline for receipt of the funds.
8. Suggest an amount they should send.
9. Give the reader one last reason for believing in The Cause and for believing the effort has a chance of succeeding.
10. Thank the reader—by name if you can do it through computer addressing—and close with the writer's name and title.

This is as complete an outline of a successful fund raising letter as can be squeezed in a book. Details of the art can be a whole career. The more you learn about it, the better you can do. And don't hesitate to tap professional help where you can—if you are certain the pros themselves are solid and effective (not all in the business are good at it). The examples at the end of this chapter are real letters that have raised thousands of dollars.

Mechanical rules for the letter:

1. Send it over the signature of the most widely known and respected citizen the group can enlist for that duty. Well-known business owners, politicians or local citizens are good choices.
2. Run the letter on excellent-quality, two-color letterhead stationery belonging to the business of the sender. Off-size personal stationery is even better.

   If the sender does not have color letterhead, consider having a commercial artist draw up stationery for the sender's company. Two-color letterhead outpulls any other by at least 1 percent. The letter signer's company (or professional affiliation for, say, a professor or physician) need not be related to the campaign.

   Stationery can be expensive. Try to get the famous person sender to donate this to the group.
3. The person sending the letter must sign each letter personally. Use a colored pen that is a different color from that of the stationery. In this and all details, strive to give the impression that the letter is individual and personalized.

   Of course for fund appeals that send out thousands of letters, it may be necessary to have the signature printed in color. You *can* ask the person to sign four or five hundred each day or until his arm falls off. Your patron may even do this, but sometimes he'll ask you if you're nuts and quit.
4. Don't worry unduly about the letter's length as long as it contains all of the necessary elements and is readable. George McGovern reportedly raised $11 million with a seven-page tome in 1972.
5. Use short quips and one-sentence paragraphs where possible in the body of the letter. No paragraph should be longer than six lines and even that is long.

6. Send the letters in company envelopes matching the letterhead on which the letter is written.

7. Always use a stamp on the envelope. Never use a postage meter unless absolutely forced to by the sheer size of a mass mailing.

8. Run each letter individually through a computer printer.

    If the size of the mailing makes this impractical, have the letters printed at a shop known for high-quality work. Lay the body of the letter out, leaving space for the internal address. Use the same printer to print the address as was used for the camera-ready copy sent to the printer. Printed on letterhead and using the same type as the address, the letter appears to be individually typed, giving the desired personalized look.

9. Type or hand-address the envelopes.

    Hand-addressed envelopes draw slightly better but seldom to the extent warranted by the extra work. Unless the group has a huge amount of volunteer labor, typing is a close second. Never use computer-generated stick-on labels.

10. Address to an individual—never to an address of the "Occupant" or to "Box Holder."

11. Include a printed return envelope in the letter. Sometimes postage-paid reply envelopes pull better, but this is not often the case and has to be tested against the considerable cost of postage and handling. Usually the convenience of having a printed address—and thus not having to write the address in responding—is far more important to the recipient than the price of a stamp. You can use a brief statement on the envelope to the effect, "Your stamp saves us money that we urgently need for the Cause."

Lists

Political Action Groups acting on solid, regional issues in which they are doing their homework will find that they receive, on the average, from two to four dollars per letter sent out if they run the formula properly and have halfway valid mailing lists.

Where does one obtain good mailing lists? During all our years in politics lists have always been forthcoming. However, the authors attach a high priority to collecting them, using vigilance always to ask people anytime there is any suspicion a list may originate with another group. It usually takes a month to six weeks but by being alert and innovative you will always have more names than you can use effectively. At the end of the campaign either sell the list or take it with you, or both.

Invariably the core group generates lists. Other associations and groups and senior citizens donate their own lists. In past campaigns, our phone rang off the hook at times with volunteers who saw a news clip on TV or in the paper and wanted to help. The first hour of every day was set aside for the clerical staff to get the new names and addresses into the computer.

One last admonition regarding *all* fund raising (not just letters). Get the requests out as early as possible. Early money has an impact four or five times greater than money late in the contest. It builds confidence and ability to persevere on the part of the group.

Sample Letter One

Mr. _____
Box _____
City, State, Zip
Dear _____:

Remember Jimmy Carter's giveaway of our Panama Canal?

Remember Jimmy Carter's four straight years of cutting defense spending? And remember our hostages in Iran?

After November 4, 1980, there will be no tomorrow. It is either Ronald Reagan or Jimmy Carter. It is Now or Never.

Mr. _____, now as never before, you have the power to shape America's future.

Don't let it be taken away from you. Don't let Jimmy Carter's distortions go without an answer.

Don't let Jimmy Carter's personal attacks on Ronald Reagan go without an answer.

Americans for Reagan must buy TV time to answer Jimmy Carter. Every American must know the Truth.

Mr. _____, I need your check for $500, $1000, $2000, $3000—even $5000—to buy TV time.

Urgent. Please—must have your answer within 48 hours. America needs Reagan. Only Good Americans like You can Make That Happen.

Please make your check out now to: Reagan TV Emergency Fund.

Remember—Tomorrow will be Too Late.

s/Senator Jesse Helms

Sample Letter Two
(Two-color stationery/letterhead. Use stamps. Sign each in blue pen.)

Dear _____:

Certainly you will agree with me that in both the short and long term, the greatest challenges facing _____ are economic.

At this moment we are in the unfortunate but correctable position of having our three economic segments in a severe depression. I don't believe industry, agriculture and service have ever in the history of our state been so simultaneously depressed.

Tourism, our only bright spot, is positive because other regions have found their way out of the morass. Their people have money to travel and are coming to _____.

There is no question that we must bite the bullet and put a team together that will lead us out of the chaos in which we now find ourselves.

That is why I am writing this letter to you today. I have decided that sitting on the sidelines and talking about our problems won't do much to solve them. I believe we must support repeal of the Compulsory Economic Review Bureau.

We haven't put it together yet in _____ but many other states have had fantastic success hiring their governor to go out and market their products. Our governor has a good plan and the necessary contacts to put this together for _____.

Winning will require a broad base of support from people like yourself but, as you well know, doing brochures in _____ is very expensive. This letter cost 27¢ for materials and 29¢ for postage. I have to mail this information to thousands like you who care about how our economic troubles harm all of us. Just one small ad in every paper in the state will cost a minimum of $18,000.

I don't know how much to ask you to send. Perhaps $100, $200, $250 or even $500.

But please act soon. As you well know, the newspapers and TV stations demand cold, hard cash before they accept any political advertising. Placement of the next, very important round of advertising is scheduled for August 17.

Regards,

Victor Raymond Farb
President of the Board
Futura Corporation

Sample Letter Three

(date)

Dear _____ Member:

I become very concerned when we residents of _____ have to rely on somebody else to do our work for us.

As you probably know, 22½ states have issued a call for a _____ to require the federal government to balance the national budget. Obviously you as an _____ member realize how important this effort is and how vital it is to stop runaway spending as well as control the many stupid federal giveaway programs we hear about every day.

However, did you know that _____ is not one of the 22 states that have done their homework and issued a _____ call? Other, far more liberal states like Delaware and Pennsylvania have come on board but _____ is still at the starting gate.

That's why I am writing you this letter.

We have an excellent chance of passing a limited state

_____ bill this session in _____.
There is an unusually competent team of business people,
legislators, attorneys, CPAs and others who have banded
together to "walk" the bill through our legislature.

In addition, we have the momentum of the _____
victory as well as a number of dedicated, committed legislators, many of whom are in places of leadership, who have
already agreed to help us.

The only thing now standing between success and
failure is support from concerned _____ citizens
like yourself.

According to our best estimates, it is going to take
about $3,500 for telephone, travel, legislative luncheons,
legal counsel, gasoline for the donated car, lodging,
postage and printing.

So far all of these expenses have either been picked up
by the core group of volunteers or by the _____.
But now we have to spread the load and help ourselves.

After all, nobody picked up the tab in the other 22
states; they did it themselves.

On January 2 the legislature goes into session. If every
one of our members in _____ dug a little deeper
and contributed just ten more dollars we could push this
project over the top.

So, please, send $10 now, or at the very latest before
January 2. Even better, send $20 or maybe even $50 to
help cover for those who have already sacrificed beyond
their limit.

As you know, the phone company and the post office
won't give credit. They demand cold, hard cash.

Thank you very much for helping with this effort. I
know with your help we'll win.

Sincerely,

Sample Letter Four

Dear Fellow _____ County Resident:

It doesn't take a very smart person to tell that we are in a heck of a mess here in _____ County.

Our tax assessment went up drastically this year. In some cases, over 300%.

Government red tape and rules are closing our industries. Factories shut down, people in the county are not working, and the Bureaucrats are even trying to stop the farmers from exporting their crop.

In our own county we have a commissioner who wants to spend-spend-spend when all of the rest of us have to cut back and watch our pennies. He appoints people to commissions and boards that do nothing but fight the average taxpaying citizen.

Our property rights are disappearing, we are billed for phony service charges and the commissioners themselves are sued almost weekly by angry residents.

That's why I have decided for the first time in my life to take drastic action and see if I can do something to help. Most of you know _____. He has lived and worked here most of his life. You know he is an intelligent, steady person who uses common sense to solve problems.

_____ has a good broad view of all our concerns. He believes in freedom and will fight to see that we keep it here in _____ County. He is a man you can rely on and trust.

Right now _____ is in a tough race with an entrenched, seasoned politician. But _____'s opponent has such a bad record we really think we have a good chance of winning. However, _____ needs your help.

He is not a wealthy man, yet he will have to spend $500 for brochures, $250 for postage, $165 for phone, $450 for gas for his car, and so on. _____ is finding that a personal commitment to good government is expensive.

Because this is a heavy load for one man, I am asking you to help. I don't know how much to ask for. Perhaps $15–$25 or even $50. Anything you send will be greatly appreciated by _____ and his committee.

Printers and the phone company will not extend credit to people like _____ who are running for public office. They demand cash.

For that reason we need to hear from you no later than September 15.

Please send your contribution to Robert Smith, _____'s campaign treasurer. With your help, I know we can win.

_____

(Signed by well known person)

Chapter 22

Mailing Lists and Direct Mail

G ood, solid, active mailing lists are the very heart and breath of any public relations/political campaign today. Twenty years ago doing the lists required typing names out on sheets of paper that we ran through a copy machine over label stock. That was a royal pain and discouraged the whole enterprise. Now we use special computer programs to group, track and sort our lists. Entry and retrieval are so easy that the process borders on the miraculous. Times change and we have to change with technology to be effective.

The first question people ask is where they can get lists, as if the lists appear by some sort of magic. Mailing lists *do* appear by magic—but the magic is the result of old-fashioned, single-minded, hard work. In brief, you generate or acquire lists by the strength of your overall appeal. The names come to you as people respond or donate their organizational lists. Those who manage political affairs will be handed the opportunity—and it is just that, for a developed list is valuable property—to put mailing lists together. With care and time, lists can be grown from almost nothing.

Nearly everything a PAG does can be a source of names. The group itself has a membership list. Members belonging to other groups may bring in those names. Use sign-up sheets at every event (meetings, rallies, speaking engagements and slide shows, county fair booths, everything), promising to send signers literature about the PAG or updates on its events. Getting addresses is the best reason to circulate petitions. Most petitions mean little to politicians and bureaucrats, but they mean a lot to the group for the names. Advertisements by the group should contain some sort of coupon so that they are a source of names. Every contact with the public is a new opportunity to add to your list. Stay alert and diligent and you will soon have a solid gold list.

Only if time is short should organizers even consider digging out or renting old, existing lists. With these, problems often arise far too often since they are old, and have not been created by *your* issue. No issues are identical, and few are similar. If you must use old lists, make sure the first mailing will identify those who are believers (and weed out those who are not) with an emotional, appeal to The Cause. It's costly but at least it's a quick entry into the list business.

Better, use seemingly unrelated but *current* lists that the group scrounges on its own. Be sure the addresses are active and up to date. The premier of these lists is the one containing all of the retirees in one's voting area. This is never an easy one to obtain. Most retiree organizations will steadfastly maintain they can never give out their lists. Officers know that retirees are targeted because they usually vote, often volunteer for and many times give money to political action projects, among other reasons. Try asking a dedicated retiree on the brain trust or in the steering committee for help acquiring this list. If that fails, try a state senator or representative. Most will have this list but will be extremely reluctant to admit that they do. The same is true with national representatives and senators. If you have a major contributor to the congressman sitting on the brain trust or board, suggest that he or she personally ask for the list.

In all cases, absolute anonymity must be extended to the list providers.

Reaching older citizens is especially important:

1. They have time to read, analyze and study the issues.
2. As a group they tend to be much more anti-government having grown up and lived with freedom.
3. Often they influence others—children and grandchildren, for instance.

4. As a group, a high percentage actually go to the polls on election day.
5. Many donate heavily to political causes.

As a result, direct mail works incredibly well with seniors. Their donations are often small, but they donate in volume.

Other, fairly productive lists, can be put together using nothing more exotic than the phone book. Often dentists, MDs and CPAs will respond to freedom-oriented issues. Try all the names once, keeping respondents on the list till it is obvious they are not replying any more.

Another group of influential individuals can be acquired from the state division of aeronautics by asking for a list of all private pilots in the region. Generally these people have high incomes as well as being hard-charging individuals. Other licensing agencies can provide highly targeted lists.

Local farm or ranch owners are often good people to target with mailings. Farmers are generally freedom-loving people who are likely to get involved in political causes if approached correctly. Local farm co-ops or farm supply stores often have fairly good mailing lists of these people.

In larger cities it is sometimes possible to buy or rent lists of potentially interested people from brokers who make it their business to provide this type of information. These businesses often are the same ones that provide district-wide mailing services.

Chambers of commerce, economic development associations, county clerks, service clubs, and sports clubs among others, are all good places to look for lists. Expect to pay between twelve and thirty cents per name at many of these organizations.

Be wary of obsolete addresses but don't overlook past political endeavors. Most communities have had a Friends of the City, Citizens United for Action or Citizens for Neutered Tomcats, etc. Some of these groups go back a number of years but their lists are often the last thing thrown out after everything else is gone. Many of these organizations are asking for more regulation or government action, limiting the value of their lists to freedom fighters. In these cases, use caution but remember the strange bedfellows rule, and be creative and open-minded.

Cataloging Your List

Careful, complete cataloging of the lists is as important as acquiring the names in the first place. Computer files should be coded so that it is an easy matter to separate out the lists based on source. It may be valuable to know if pilots, doctors, CPAs, retired people or whatever are the most frequent responders to the group's plight. If the mailing is to Mr. and Mrs., keep track of who in the family has the greater interest. Track by age and sex if possible, as well as income (if known), area of residence, past political affiliation and any other demographic data that may be helpful. Even such things as rural vs. city, zip codes and children in school may be helpful to the campaign.

In all cases it is absolutely vital that the files be coded to show who received what mailings including the date and who gave how much to the campaign. Exact amounts collected should be carefully coded after every name. Keep track of what device triggered the donation—letter, brochure, call, attendance at a meeting, newspaper article, paid ad or whatever, if known.

Standard today is to generate by computer a thank-you letter tailored to the content and form of the original prompting request. If the numbers are not forbidding, pen a short personal note on the bottom of the letter to be included in the mailing of the receipt.

No matter what the group's circumstances, a high priority absolutely must be placed on keeping the group's lists current. The first staff items each day should involve updating and coding the new names acquired by the group. Besides lists for targeted mailings, separate lists should be kept of campaign supporters. Often people volunteer to do special work on political projects. This can include working at polling, literature distribution, designing brochures, being part of the speakers bureau, clerical duties in the office or any one of hundreds of other chores. Code the computer files showing who has volunteered to do what. Finding people for a slot becomes much easier, and volunteers do not inadvertently drop out of the system if computer files are properly maintained. In a business where timing and expedience are vital, being able instantly to pull up lists of potential callers or envelope addressers gives the campaign a huge advantage.

In contrast to specific, targeted direct mail, blanketed direct mail is seen by experienced politicians as being the wave of the future. Initial mailings to names on purchased or scrounged mailing lists should be viewed as targeted in nature, done to see if these people have more than passive interest in the group's issues. After the campaign matures, it may be appropriate to get out additional specific targeted letters or brochures to previously identified classes of people—i.e., the doctors may get one letter, the workers at the factory another, and so on—and to do mass mailings of brochures to everyone in the county, city or region. These regional mailings can be extremely potent. However, they are too advanced for any but established, sizable and experienced PAGs, so are largely beyond the scope of this book.

In larger cities, direct mail providers exist who will handle everything. If desired, they will design and print the group's mailing literature and have postage permit numbers that the group can use. Compare services and expenses, for mailing, design and printing, before committing to a professional mailer.

The strength of direct mail is to target specific pre-identified areas with specific issues. An ideal format for brochures that are to be mailed (usually not the same as handouts or fact sheets) is to list current opposition charges one by one, then refute them with good, solid arguments from the brain trust or based on polls. As a general rule, do not try to cover more than five issues in a single mailing and do not format the brochure larger than a single legal-sized sheet of paper folded twice.

A quality brochure on coated paper, professionally printed goes a long way toward giving the group credibility and of securing voter support. Direct mail brochures are excellent places to display artists' sketches or photos. Effective brochures can be done by skilled volunteers, but such talents are not common.

Professional, bulk mailers charge about twenty to twenty-five cents per piece mailed. They will know exactly how many names they have for each region, and can quote exact prices by area. Smart mailers will sit down with you to evaluate their services, vis-à-vis what the polls suggest are the weak places in the campaign. Theoretically these are the places where direct mail money would be most effectively spent. Reputable mailers will set an exact date for the mailing and always meet it if you have all the material in their hands on time.

A few especially aggressive direct mail firms have some very useful targeted lists they can sell, other than regional lists. These might include names of all doctors, teachers, retirees, or whatever. They may even be able to supply everyone in the county who registered as a Republican in the last election, or everyone on Harrison Street or everyone on Harrison and Elm streets. If the group's needs seem profitable to them, many direct mail concerns will assemble customized lists of desired names and addresses. It always pays to ask.

Direct mail is a hardball tactic that more freedom fighters should be using. Often it will identify financial supporters who, in turn, cover the cost of the mailing. With that kind of success you roll out your mailings and grow quickly into a political force to be reckoned with.

Chapter 23

Newsletters and Political Speeches

Newsletters and political speeches are cousins in the business of getting the word out. Speeches get the troops in the field excited and involved while newsletters keep them in the game. Like much in politics, both are done by formula.

The formulas in these cases are not particularly difficult to learn and implement. The only intangible is speech delivery. Some people speak well while others have trouble with public speaking.

President Kennedy had what was acknowledged as the best speech writing staff in modern American politics. He was also one of the most articulate, quick-witted men to come along since Winston Churchill. President Reagan is contemporarily known as the Great Communicator. He also had an excellent staff of writers as well as great experience and training as an actor. Great speakers have great staff and vice versa.

It is by no means insulting to note that even President Reagan with all his great skill, experience and staff, used the standard political speech formula every time he spoke. In his hands it became an art form. But the formula is excellent in itself and should not be taken lightly.

Universally, political speeches start off with a recitation recognizing every person at the meeting with whom that politician has ever had any contact: "I am happy to see my good friends Ralph Smith and Phil Latta among you today," or "Being back in River City is always a pleasure because I can check on the news with my good old friend Dennis Coon. We sure have been to the wars together, haven't we, Dennis?" These recognitions are filled in at the very last minute, often with the help of the politician's staff or with the president of the assembled group.

If it appears that there are embarrassingly few locals to recognize, the smart politician will recognize other politicians. By so doing the politician identifies with local people and subtly makes them his supporters. If all else fails, the speaker can recognize club VPs who have no choice but to be in the audience.

The next item in the speech is to list everything that the politician has ever done for members of that group, or for the community. Professional staffers write this portion of the speech and they tend to be pretty inventive about the things the boss supposedly accomplished. Some of these great achievements, you can bet, were simply not handled by that legislator, or were done contrary to his best efforts to stop them, or even may be things the legislator blocked. But the list is important and it is firmly worked out and written down, not subject to last-minute changes.

The body of the speech should cover the points that the congressman's polls, local staff or brain trust indicates are of prime interest to the audience. This changes dramatically from area to area and over time. Congressmen expend considerable effort keeping up on these local issues.

The body of the speech must contain a number of quotable comments—now called sound bites—related to the pertinent issues. These are the portions of the speech picked up by the media that are often quoted over and over. Writers slave over the wording because of the potential for repetition. It is always amazing to discover how often the same hot quotes are applied to a wide range of issues.

Quotable comments are easy for some people. Mark Twain, for instance, spun out pithy little sayings about virtually everything. Most of us are not Mark Twains but merely knowing that sound bites are needed is half the answer. We can look for help in a book of quotations—any good library will offer many of them—or better, tailor existing proven winners. Twain's own comment that "A gold mine is a hole in the ground with a liar standing next to it" can be used in dozens of different contexts. Modify it, for instance, to read, "An EPA bureaucrat is a liar complaining about garbage because he wants to charge us an arm and a leg to haul it away." If you're not satisfied with one result, flip it around and try another: "A pile of garbage is a race between maggots looking for food and an EPA bureaucrat looking for a pay raise."

The body of the speech is a simple recitation of the issues as the group sees them. Detail the *W*'s of enemy villainy: who has done what to whom, and when. Include a summary of the group's position along with pertinent statistics supporting it. Be sure listeners have no illusion regarding the group's purpose and goals. Sprinkle your hot quotes liberally through the material. As a rule, more problems arise from trying to be too brief in this section rather than from stretching it enough to make your whole case.

The conclusion of the speech must be upbeat. Depending on your theme, close with a laugh or a message of inspiration that will move the audience to future action. As any good sales call ends by asking for the order, a political speech should conclude with a special call to arms. For example, "Vote for me," or "Your financial help is urgently needed to buy TV spots," or "Say no to their outrageous, expensive, freedom-robbing programs." Go over this part with special care to get as much power and uplift and appeal as you can into the wording.

The length for a speech depends on circumstances. But one big consideration today is TV. Most speakers try to do the job in a framework suitable for a half-hour TV time slot. But there are no final rules. Fidel Castro is famous for rambling speeches to the faithful that go on for as long as four hours. Skilled speakers read the crowd, continuing as long as they can stay in control and build the hysteria.

Have a dolled-up, sanitized version of the speech ready to hand out to the media as soon as the speaker is done. Even if the speaker didn't actually get around to saying some of the things in this version, the material in desired form should be instantly available to interested supporters and others, along with the media.

Newsletters

Our Side has not taken enough advantage of newsletters, much to the detriment of our projects. The group's newsletter is a periodic reminder to members about the issues, and hence keeps them committed and active. It is equally useful for news flashes, issue updates, "personal" messages from the leaders and calls for action.

Our rule of thumb is that if the project will run more than six months we budget for and get out a monthly newsletter. Sending out a newsletter every thirty days, to be sure, takes a tremendous commitment of staff time, money for postage, paper and production. But without the newsletter you risk losing track of your supporters and having them lose interest in the cause that brought them together.

Naming the newsletter is always a challenge. Creativity and catchiness pay big dividends. Trust in your brain trust! Open the subject to debate. You can (and must) do better than the River City Action Report, or any name people can't remember.

The first newsletter mailing can be the news release announcing the formal launching of the Political Action Group. The second month's mailing could be little more than the fact sheet, jazzed up for internal consumption. Assuming a six-month campaign, that leaves four more mailings that some creative hack will have to write. These subsequent newsletters can be filled with editorials, news about recent group activities, meeting announcements, copies of letters to and from bureaucrats, facts, figures and arguments along with pertinent quotes.

New arguments and facts regarding the issues and objectives should be included as they arise. At times it may be necessary to get out a special newsletter, if events are breaking rapidly. When the brain trust comes up with new, innovative ideas regarding how issues should be addressed, put a clip in the sheet advising the troops. Similarly, newsletters are your means to sound the alarm. No matter how many times a group has announced the impending death of the World's Last Blue Whale, or Redwood Tree, it always seems to work.

Group newsletters structured to keep current members active and involved in something less than crisis situations contain huge amounts of insider news about what is being done to further the cause. These will include details concerning news conferences, slide show schedules, attendance at rallies, featured speakers, endorsements and general plans for the future. The most important single element of these newsletters is a detailed, exact recitation of what the group has been doing and who exactly has been doing it. Get in all the names that you can—column after column of them, if necessary. Put a fund appeal of some sort in every issue, too. Don't expect the newsletter to finance any other activity but it can bring in enough contributions to pay for itself, and that is a great relief to your budget.

Small personal newsletters must be exactly that—news. They should be written to include news not available in the papers or on TV. This is often much easier said than done unless the group is fortunate enough to have a veteran newsletter writer in its midst.

Every copy of the newsletter should be routinely sent to members of the media. Under these circumstances mention of a politician or bureaucrat in a favorable way is a plus for the group. Officials who know they may be praised or criticized in a newsletter tend to deal with the group more kindly. Should someone from the media prove to be especially disreputable when dealing with the group, the newsletter provides a means of chastising that person and setting the record straight. Media people hate this device to the point of being very wary of it.

Do not use the regular stock newsletter sheet for action alerts. Instead, get out an SOS sheet printed in bright red or white paper containing nothing but the news that open warfare has erupted, we need help, or whatever.

Simple set-ups for the newsletter are all but essential. A satisfactory expedient is to preprint blank, two-color newsletter stationery that can be filled with current news items. Once typed on the newsletter form, any quick print shop can inexpensively produce a plate that will run up to several thousand newsletters on the stock stationery. This allows for classy two-color formats that attract people's attention.

Artistically inclined group supporters have done some very creative work blending group logos, colored paper and contrasting colored stock ink. One never knows when people with these skills will materialize out of what seems like thin air. We can say that these skills, and the right hardware, are easier to find every day. The ubiquitous personal computer and the laser printer are ideal for low-resolution printing appropriate to newsletters. Along with publishing software, they are easy enough to use so that ordinary office help, writers and wannabes, and political activists have the ability to generate type, layouts and even graphs and line-art in house.

At this writing the cheapest method of sending newsletters through the postal service is via a bulk-rate postage permit. Cost is about 16.7 cents per piece mailed. The individual pieces can weigh up to 3½ ounces each. The postal service also has nonprofit rates that allow one to mail for as low as 8.4 cents per piece. Qualifying for the nonprofit rate is tricky and uncertain, so have it checked by an attorney. For most politically active groups, the not-for-profit status may not be worth the savings in postage. Postal regulations must be checked also. Additional cost reductions are granted for additional work performed on the mailing such as sorting by zip code and by carrier route. Cost can drop from 16.7 cents to about 13.2 cents per piece mailed, or even less in some cases.

The entire newsletter effort must, by nature, be a staff production and a focus for the group. It is a nearly indispensable means of assuring the membership that the body is doing the right thing at the right time. That is exactly what you need to keep going and growing.

Chapter 24

Demonstrations

Demonstrations—including the picketing kind and mass rallies—are valuable when the strategy suggests that a strong immediate public statement is appropriate. They are difficult to organize properly, but when done correctly they can give the group more instant public visibility than could otherwise be generated by virtually any other method.

On the other hand, demonstrations can constitute real dangers for the group if they are improperly done. This is especially true when the media are hostile toward the goals and purposes of the organizing group. One can count on the media being hostile toward any group advocating a free-market approach to problems at least 80 percent of the time.

Demonstrations can be an ideal vehicle for use by tiny Political Action Groups. It takes very few people to demonstrate successfully. By definition, a demonstration causes controversy. If all the group has at its command are six or eight volunteers, they are easily sufficient to make the evening news. Numbers are usually less important than that the organizers and the foot soldiers agree why they are in the streets. In all cases the action should dovetail with the overall group strategy. If this initial starting point cannot be reached, demonstrations should not be attempted.

When the purpose of the action is decided, the participants must be thoroughly briefed. It is necessary for them to know what specific evil they protest. There should be a special fact sheet for the participants. This document should not be confused with the prepared statement distributed to the media. Mark them clearly and distribute them correctly.

Tell the demonstrators about the prepared news release and, if absolutely necessary, use the main group fact sheet if a special Demonstrator Edition cannot be produced. What they need in this case are background facts and figures that reinforce their resolve to get out and make a spectacle of themselves and to answer briefly if reporters do question them.

An excellent time for demonstrators to do their instructional homework is at a predemonstration get-together when the signs are hammered together and painted. Handled properly, the exercise is a wonderful morale booster for the group.

A favorite trick when organizing counterdemonstrations—and beware of it being used against you—is to lead the media over to an opposition member who is inarticulate and unsure why he or she is there. The results are often devastating when the opposition organizers do not do their homework and the demonstrator provides a bumbling, rambling, illogical monologue.

Demonstrations, in the final analysis, are organized for the benefit of the media. Evening news deadlines must always be a major consideration when putting people in the streets. Organizers who have not worked extensively with the media and who know them well, should be wary of trying to put demonstrations together unassisted. Bureaucrats are often devastated when the media call an hour before the demonstration to ask, for example, "Did you know that there is going to be a demonstration in opposition to your asbestos policy?" The impact is so great it provides one of the true highs that this business can provide.

The most convincing demonstrators are otherwise respectable citizens—farmers, mothers with baby strollers, seniors—who seem slightly out of place, and precisely because of it, convey that they have a real grievance. For similar reasons, homemade signs that are a bit amateurish-looking draw greater sympathy and identification when seen on TV. They must be done in blacks, reds and blues so as to show up well. Other colors do not show up as well on TV.

Reporters sometimes cause problems by asking children in the demonstration questions. The best method of handling what could be an embarrassing situation is to have the group spokesman call all the media about two hours before the event. Tell them what will happen, where it will happen and a bit about the group. Keep this backgrounding to a minimum. Include only enough information so that the newsroom can relate to it previous events. If things go well, by the time the group starts demonstrating media people will know the group spokesman, and the group itself, by sight.

It also helps to tell the media there are several excellent spokesmen available who will leave the group for a few moments to be interviewed. By using this device it is possible to steer the media over to your more articulate people. Make extensive use of prepared press releases given to the media and to interested onlookers.

East of the Mississippi, most cities require advance notice and, in some cases, permits for demonstrations. West of the river things are a bit more relaxed. Be sure to check.

Places where demonstrations are held are as important as when and should be part of the gimmick the group employs. Pick spots the media can easily cover. As much as is humanly possible, try not to schedule a demonstration on a big news day or on holidays or in circumstances that would make coverage difficult (during rush hour, for example). Always check the wire service daybook.

Carefully plan out the route the demonstrators will take. Let them know where to park, when to meet and what to bring. Novices even need to know what to wear. It is especially helpful to let participants know when the event will be over, or to have some prearranged signal to wrap it up. Wise political operatives keep demonstrations under maximum control.

Rallies are the kind of demonstration where as a rule you deploy a speaker. Should the group have the good fortune to be able to enlist the services of a visiting celebrity who has unusual rhetorical ability, a rally can be extremely effective. A second essential element of a successful rally is that the group maintains absolute control of the public address system and that the system be significantly more powerful than anything one's opponents might roll onto the scene.

Don't ever, ever consider being fair and even-handed by inviting the opposition onto your platform so that both sides of the issue can be explored. Counterdemonstrations directed against rallies are only effective if the demonstrators can be heard and if they are successful in siphoning off media folk who will listen to their arguments.

Rallies are only effective if the group is 100 percent certain that they can attract a large enough crowd to be credible. Size of the crowd, in this case, is vitally important. That's why we speak of "mass" rallies. The group will have to analyze each situation in order to decide if it is in danger of being too small to make an impact.

Unlike demonstrations and rallies, picketing implies a long-term commitment. Pickets are set up in response to an injustice. They should not be removed until the injustice is remedied. The only exception is to embarrass a congressman or chief bureaucrat or other VIP who visits a regional office for a day. It is a good means of making a statement directly to these people.

Whatever is done, put the group's best effort into making the event clever, colorful and out of the ordinary. Dramatics count in this process. The brain trust should work overtime to come up with demonstration gimmicks. The only real limitation is on the cleverness of the organizers. Pro-life demonstrators traditionally pass out fresh roses as they go through their routine. In another case, EPA administrators who thought up impossible, costly rules for communities were handed fresh lemons. Once author Steve Symms mailed fresh potatoes to each senator as an Idaho allegory for an economic recovery bill under consideration: if the senators didn't do anything, the mess would rot on their desks!

Chapter 25

Going to Jail

Going to jail can generate quicker and cheaper publicity than virtually any other method involving so few people. But it is, after all, going to jail, and no matter how hot we may be about our issue, we have to weigh that kind of decision with extra caution.

Historically people in our country have gone to jail over civil rights issues and in an attempt to end our various wars. In its way, this is media theater and it plays on the public's sense of justice. In successful efforts a broad base of popular support or sympathy existed for the protesters' point of view. Today it is hard to imagine an issue that has sufficiently popular support to make going to jail effective from a public relations standpoint.

Unlike many of history's most infamous leaders—Lenin, Adolf Hitler, Mao Tse-tung and Ho Chi Minh, for instance—the fathers of our country, Washington, Jefferson, Franklin and all, did their work without doing time. The democratic citizen is as a rule law-abiding; a respect for freedom keeps him out of jail. The people with whom we have traditionally worked would find going to jail to be worrisome at best and far outside their experience. Suggesting that they go out and get arrested is "making pigs fly," in the worst possible circumstances.

However, Martin Luther King, Jr. often used the device of being thrown into prison to build membership among potential supporters and to raise money. Cottonbrained southern sheriffs played into his hand as if they were on the man's payroll. King got TV and newspaper opportunities that would never have been available to him under other circumstances, or by any other method. He seldom spent more than a day or two in custody.

We hear many of our thoroughly fed-up activist friends say that we should go out, demonstrate, trespass, and get thrown into the joint for the Good of the Cause. We would caution otherwise but can at least imagine situations in which going to jail might be the right tactic. It is also possible that the present mood would change to one more in need of drastic measures.

In every case if one intends to go to jail, arrangements should be made for an absolute avalanche of publicity relative to the event. It does very little good to go to jail, for instance, if one fails to make the front page of the papers in the process.

The general rule of thumb is that two to a maximum of thirty days is the most jail time a political activist had better sign up for. After thirty days have elapsed, most supporters in the United States tend to lose track of why their people went to jail in the first place. The cause can easily get stuck in the mud and start to founder if the leaders are out of circulation longer than about four weeks.

Tax protesters especially should beware, because they usually draw very long sentences for relatively minor infractions. One fellow who was found in contempt of court on a tax matter was allowed to rot in prison for over a year by an especially motivated judge. The device worked because there was no one on the outside beating the drum for the poor man. He might as well have dropped into a black hole. Out of sight and forgotten, he was unable even to continue his work as a protester. The same thing can happen to home schoolers, who simply go off to jail for contempt of court.

Be sure if you, as an activist, are going to jail, that you:

1. Dress simply in reasonably dressy yet modest clothes. (Keep in mind that your clothes may be ruined.) The dilemma is to look good on TV and in photos while being reasonably comfortable in the lockup. Protesters must look like the average citizen with whom they are trying to identify.
2. Take along any prescription drugs that you may require. Your jailers will hold these, dispensing them on the prescribed schedule.
3. Take along a small amount of cash to use for phone calls and

to buy candy and sundries from the commissary. Contrary to popular opinion, this money, if the amount is modest, is not likely to be stolen except, perhaps, in the larger, less-well-run big-city jails.

4. Provide yourself with certain necessaries. Jailers are obligated to provide toothbrushes and soap, but experienced protesters suggest slipping these items in their pockets before heading off to the slammer.

5. If possible, take along some reading material. There will be little to nothing available where you are going.

Arrests should always be for relatively minor misdemeanors such as public disturbance, trespassing or public nuisance. Do not ever hit a policeman, destroy government or private property, or get arrested while carrying any weapon and/or controlled substance. These offenses are felonies and different, much more stringent rules apply.

No matter what the group decides about including going to jail in its strategy, make sure it is your personal decision and not the authorities making it for you. Tax protesters who are suddenly and unexpectedly dragged off kicking and screaming on a charge of contempt of court don't make much of a political point. You go to jail, if at all, to make a statement, so pick the circumstances yourself. Jail is twice as bad if you can't make your point and could be doing more harm to the bureaucracy on the outside.

Chapter 26

Producing a Campaign Brochure

ost political campaigns require a brochure as a sales tool. As a rule of thumb, brochures are needed in all partisan campaigns and at least half of initiative/issue campaigns. If the brochure is to the point and pleasingly designed, it is always a plus, "needed" or not. Some campaigns require a succession of brochures.

Brochures are used as get-acquainted literature, fund raising devices, and educational tools. They can serve the purpose of a handbill—to mobilize people to vote, and at the same time be a mini-guidebook—explaining difficult-to-understand, convoluted issues so that the troops will know how to vote right. Brochures can use photos or pictures to demonstrate issues in a manner not otherwise available to the Political Action Group.

The principal purpose for issuing a succession of brochures is keeping abreast of changing issues as identified by one's polls and by the brain trust. To a limited extent, one must counter the charges of an opponent. Issue-oriented campaigns appealing to the court of public opinion require from one to three brochures, depending on how much the public perception needs to be changed and to what extent the issue may evolve. Depending on the length of the campaign, it is best to figure on two or three different brochures. Better too many than too few, and lose the contest.

Two important brochure-related issues come into view at this point. On the one hand, every charge must be answered. Yet, as a rule, successful campaigns do not spend their time countering the charges of the opposition. Instead, the campaign should always attempt to make the opposition address our issues and the trends that are sweeping them along. No candidate's brochure, issue brochure or any other type of brochure should ever be negative or reactive except in the most carefully considered manner. It is also advisable not to dwell on past abuses other than to the extent required to get the troops in the field. Opponents of excessive government have a propensity to recite long lists of the black depravity of the bureaucracy, without including any mitigating plans of action or hope for the future. These litanies vent frustration but they do not convince the uncommitted.

Using the brain trust and polls, questions can be addressed, or in some cases raised, in a purely positive way and without hinting at being reactionary. Ways in which questions are answered often carry more impact than what is actually said.

Brochures must evolve with the campaign so as continually to address the new issues. Each new one must look different from the last so that the reader will know that it's new (something that he or she hasn't read yet). Yet the brochures should always contain some unique group "signature" such as color, type style, paper texture, or logo that identifies it with the PAG. It is important that when the instant recipients pick up the brochure, they know (or cannot mistake) that it is *yours.* For example, you might do this by using the same format or the same dramatic logo, but switch the color of the ink to "announce" psychologically that this is a new publication with a new subject. Periodicals often use this easy trick.

Some smaller campaigns don't even need a brochure. If funds are not available and if the issues do not warrant a full-blown campaign, a little fact sheet often works nicely. But a lack of time, money and skill to produce a brochure should never become an excuse to do a less than 100 percent job on any campaign. Even the tree huggers and the antifarmer groups get out some kind of printed material that they can use to tell their story and perhaps raise a few dollars.

Before the campaign starts in earnest, it is difficult to impossible to know what actual issues should be dealt with in one's printed literature. For this reason, it is important that the brochures not be assembled too early. By the time that a brain trust has been established and the group has succeeded in getting out a competent fact sheet, you are probably ready to start in earnest on the PAG brochure. Expect to spend forty to sixty hours of staff time assembling a brochure, especially when pictures must be taken.

Creating the Brochure

Before you write one word, understand the format you'll be writing in. It is nearly standard that brochures be made up on a single sheet of 8½ x 11 or 8½ x 14 paper. The paper is folded twice producing six panels. Inside the panels can be doubled if need be, producing one large picture with a crease in it. Special situations sometimes dictate other paper sizes and formats, but for now count on using this one. An 8½ x 11 sheet of paper can be folded so as to fit in a standard number 10 envelope. An 8½ x 14 sheet is best designed as a self-mailer, sacrificing one panel on the brochure. Successful brochures have been developed on a sheet of 8½ x 6 paper folded once or on a standard sheet folded in half. No set rule exists. Do whatever appears to be the most effective, given the copy at hand.

Next, notice that brochures are a graphics medium (pictures). Forgetting the old saw that a picture is worth a thousand words, most amateur brochures are needlessly detailed and complex. You want to get all the clout you can out of your photos. This means you'll use relatively few words and will want to leave white space to make the pictures even more dramatic. And after all, you can't put all that many words on a single sheet of paper, even printed on both sides.

With these considerations in mind, we are ready to look at the job of writing and putting together the brochure. To some extent both kinds of campaign brochures (those for candidates and those for initiatives or issue campaigns) are done by formula. There is a measure of artistic skill involved that takes the process out of the paint-by-number category, but several guidelines apply.

First, collect a number of related brochures from which to pick up ideas. Your printshop may have a file of them. It is easy to copy the layout of one that you like. You can learn from others' mistakes too. Note features that you don't like, talk over why they don't appeal, and then avoid that feature or technique.

What dictates content is that campaigns settle out to a few main issues (if they don't shake out, pick the top issues and stick to those). Address these key issues with pictures, graphs and a few words of explanation. Brochures are one of the few methods by which the general public can be alerted as to what the candidates and families look like, what the candidate does for a living, where he went to school, and so on. The right picture tells all that, or how he stands on issues. (If the candidate is against gun-control laws, get a photo of the candidate hunting.) Initiative campaigns showing kids in a private school, businesses boarded up, jobs lost, people hungry because farm crops were wasted, are all wonderfully effective.

Panel one should provide the hook, drawing the reader into the brochure. Partisan candidates do this with pictures and a simple statement. "John Smith for U.S. Congress." Some add that they are incumbent, Republican or Democrat. Initiative campaigns may have a title listing the name of the Political Action Group and then a catchy explanation of what the group wants. This explanation must be general in nature yet framed in terms meaningful and motivating to the average voter.

Names such as "Citizens Associated to Defeat Initiative 17" are not nearly as dramatic as "Citizens to Stop School Board Waste." If possible, use rhetoric that emphasizes threats to the potential readers, such as losing their jobs. For instance: "How you vote Tuesday, May 22, will determine if you have a job (educate your kids, keep a cat, etc.)." Many issue-oriented campaigns can employ their own version of the polarizing statement, "What the bureaucrats in Washington, D.C. want is not good for River City."

Inside the brochure, draw the readers into the political fray quickly with a succinct statement framing the issue. Make sure your PAG's position is icy clear. Insofar as one accurately can, ignore any argument on the other side of the issue. If possible, use quotes from other sources to polarize the reader.

Like the fact sheet before, a brochure must focus on the exact reasons the Political Action Group exists and needs to take action. Make the photos the center of attention and let them carry the load. Keep the written material simple, keep it brief. Be as forceful as the brain trust and polls allow, but without becoming negative.

Conclude the brochure with a specific, positive call to action. Wise political operatives sometimes get two pleas in for the price of one. They can ask for both action and financial help by saying, "Please help—with your time or a contribution." The group may get both. In any case, there must be no question in the reader's mind what he needs to do.

Production

Unless your group has prior experience, tough tasks await you in the production of a brochure. Getting the content and copy right is just the beginning. The mechanical layout—including print style, size, color, and paper stock—poses technical problems that a novice group will need help to solve. The best way of evaluating what can be done is to ask an older, full-service print shop to pull from its files examples of clever jobs it has previously run. Specify that you want to unite the paper texture, color of ink and type of pictures in a coherent whole. Your library will have several guidebooks to help staff members assigned to these chores. The more they can learn in advance, the better.

The brochure should not look cheap or shoddy. Even if done with black ink and white paper, use heavier cover stock rather than light mimeo grade paper. In as many cases as money will allow, consider using heavier grades of coated paper.

After the copy has been set and fitted into the brochure space, the printer will set up a proof, or first draft of the actual layout of the brochure. As a rule of thumb, the material from which this is developed should have been circulated among the brain trust and board of directors for comment.

At the proof stage, you can't have too many people look at a brochure. Credibility-destroying typos and misspellings seem to creep in no matter how hard one tries to keep them out. Do your level best to keep errors out (but don't be surprised when they show up anyway). Ask an outside professional to proofread your copy when your staff is done with it.

All material that might be mailed should contain the group's bulk mailing permit number.

Huge technological leaps in desktop publishing have made the production of a brochure both quick and relatively inexpensive. We find (year-end, 1993) that brochures have been running about $175 per 500 or $225 per 1,000. Expect to pay about $30 per 1,000 after the first 1,000. "Quick" printing is good up to about 7,000 brochures, in our experience. After that the printing plates start to deteriorate. You should use a "regular" printer (the technique is different) when a higher number of brochures is being prepared. In this case, set-up charges are higher, but the run charges are lower so that you start saving money in larger print runs, perhaps at 18,000 or 20,000 copies.

All this may seem terribly complicated but it gets easier with a bit of experience and there are no insurmountable problems. Just plain folks put out thousands of campaign brochures every year, and you can too. You can get all sorts of how-to help at libraries, at printshops, at mailing houses or through agencies that specialize in direct mail. Hammer your issues, present them in a way that is pleasing to your eye, and you've created a brochure that will help win the fight to restore liberty.

Chapter 27

How Bureaucrats Think, Live and Work

E arly on Sunday, December 7, 1941, Bruce Kirchner decided to take advantage of nice weather and a quiet, uneventful day to catch up on a bit of hedge trimming at his assigned garden area. Kirchner, then a buck private in the army, enjoyed his solitary duties as grounds tender for the flower gardens surrounding Hickam Air Field. It was a peaceful job, providing as much satisfaction as a rural farm boy from Idaho was likely to find in Hawaii.

At about 7:15 A.M. Mr. Kirchner began to hear the low, throaty rumble of large numbers of powerful airplanes. He vividly recalls wondering about the number of engines required to generate so much noise. Soon the ground he stood on shook as high-powered Japanese Zero fighters and Nakajima torpedo bombers lumbered over, so low he could count the rivets. The thumping of expending ordnance in the harbor told him that this was no routine fly by.

The twenty-four-year-old volunteer sprinted to a small tool shed where he kept the lawn mowers, hedge clippers, rakes and a World War I Springfield bolt action rifle. Private possession of a working firearm was strictly illegal even fifty years ago in Hawaii. His little hoard of live ball ammo—thirteen rounds, he recalls fondly—was hidden carefully with the pirated rifle under a number of clay pots and bales of burlap.

Back at the edge of the airfield, Bruce took slow, deliberate aim at the lumbering torpedo bombers flying a scant 150 feet over his head. Poor farm boys raised as hunters know how to conserve their ammunition. To this day Kirchner is certain he holed at least a half

136

dozen of the enemy aircraft by the time he fired his last round.

During a lull, Kirchner ran over to the hangar area to see if he could find some ammunition. Several supply sergeants were at or near their posts at the airfield arms rooms. Kirchner and other GIs begged for weapons, but no matter how much they threatened or cursed, these hardened old bureaucrats refused to turn over arms or ammunition without "proper authorization."

Readers who are familiar with a bureaucracy or who have worked in one might ask, "So what is amiss? You have to go by the rules. There are always authorizations needed, papers to fill out, and countersignatures to secure. The sergeants were just doing their jobs and doing them right." And that is exactly correct. From their own view, the bureaucrats' actions were not only excusable but necessary. There is an ever-useful lesson in this for the rest of us, who see how idiotic it was to keep our guns under lock and key while Pearl Harbor was under attack.

Freedom fighters must learn and never forget that we are at war with a bureaucratic enemy who thinks exactly as those supply sergeants did at Hickam Field. It oughtn't to be much of a problem to deal with such rigid, bureaucratic thinking, but demonstrably it is. The bureaucracy is a pervasive, daunting problem for most active, goal-oriented, entrepreneurial Americans. By its very nature the bureaucracy will always think of reasons why a given thing must be done by the rules or not done at all. Bureaucrats exist to say no. If they control the situation, they will not act unless one follows their exact procedures.

In real life the toughest, most intransigent bureaucracies have such inherent weaknesses that Our Side should always prevail. Obviously this is not the case. We continually lose battles that should have been no contest, because we fail to understand and exploit their weakness!

Know your enemy! We must spend more time analyzing our adversaries with the intent of using the tactics found elsewhere in this book. Not all bureaucrats operate exactly in the manner described below. Enough do, however, so that freedom fighters should seriously look in these areas for assailable weaknesses.

As the incident in Hawaii amply demonstrates, bureaucracies assume that any excuse for doing nothing is ten times better than taking an action that might fall outside their normal operating procedure. People likely to take these jobs are comfortable being a small cog in a very large machine. They are super team players but timid and unambitious. Nobody goes into a bureaucracy out of burning desire to make a mark on the world. Rather, they seek the job security, all-but-guaranteed advancement, and relatively easy money of an undemanding job. They like not having to take risks or make decisions.

The timidity of bureaucrats and the rigid rules under which they operate are handicaps that freedom fighters can take advantage of. Where bureaucrats dawdle and shrink from initiative, Our Side is flexible, enterprising and fast. Agencies are expert at trying to force citizens to pay their fines or adhere to their rules, but get them even a little outside their area and it becomes an entirely new game. Bureaucrats work in situations where their jobs are tightly defined by their job descriptions and cannot relate or do much of anything outside of the defined role. This is just the moment to put them in the glare of the spotlight and demand action or decisions. Publicity is their nightmare and our goal.

Agency people, as a group, fear publicity as much as they fear operating without rules and procedures. Bureaucrats have been known to need therapy simply because their names appeared in the papers or in the evening TV news, even though the mention was favorable. Advancement in an agency depends on longevity, a low profile, and *not rocking the boat*. Bureaucrats whose actions are publicly questioned may see all chance for rapid advancement go instantly out the window, and their terror in these situations cannot be overestimated.

Freedom fighters must use whatever means possible including the Freedom of Information Act (FOIA), past agency employers, personal experience, congressional staff, spies, attorneys, other past victims, and so on, to find out everything possible about the operating procedures of an offending agency. Every piece of information must be carefully evaluated and filed in an attempt to determine if it might constitute the rope with which one will hang that bureaucrat.

While doing this, remember that we should always operate within our own frame of reference and outside the opposition's. It is easy enough in most cases, for freedom fighters will find that the bureaucracy operates in a narrow spectrum of allowable initiatives. If we are motivated and clever about always forcing the bureaucrat to choose between following the rules (which he badly wants to do) and making an independent decision (which he cannot do), we will win every time, or close to it. At times it isn't easy but we can still be innovative when the bureaucracy never can.

Our frame of reference starts with realizing that our freedom has been infringed by the bureaucracy's rules, and we aim to get it back. Citizen groups often feel ashamed of what the agencies were doing *to* them, thinking they, the citizens, had broken some moral, ethical or perhaps a political rule. They should have realized that they were the victims of a bureaucratic grab at their freedoms! They should have rushed to a news conference prompting the news people to start prowling up and down the musty halls of the agencies. Instead, they held back, thinking that perhaps they actually were the offenders, and lost the fight.

Freedom fighting groups that have gained a reputation for fighting a loud, rough, fight in the media will be avoided by the agencies at all cost. But first the group must hammer the bureaucracy hard at least once. In this case, an overreaction can be a virtue.

To make matters easier for Our Side, the agencies virtually never know how to deal with the media. They don't know how to dress, how to hold news conferences—assuming their rules would allow them the luxury of organizing a news conference—or how to get out news releases. The very best they could hope for is that their regional headquarters would send out a PR man. Asking for PR help constitutes boat rocking at its worst. Agency people will always be reluctant to take this step.

For no good reason news people generally favor regulation of everything (but reporters). Yet they seem to detest their brothers in the bureaucracy. Do a halfway intelligent, credible job of holding a news conference, getting out a news release, writing a brochure, etc., and we will have their ear and probably at least their tacit support.

News conferences naming names are dynamite, but pickets in front of a bureau are an atom bomb. Especially if those inside are busy filling time-consuming FOIA requests. Freedom fighters who doubt the above should try suing individual bureaucrats by name. If the group resources are limited, do it in small claims court. At the news conference announcing the suit, the media may not differentiate between district court and small claims court. If the media know the difference, the general public will not, and for sure the bureaucrats' bosses will not.

Most importantly, draw up the papers, do the needed homework and sue. Sue them for alleged damages, for FOIA violations, to see material files, but sue. Get individual bureaucrats' names in print. Clip the items from the paper or make a videotape and send it to your U.S. senators and to the agency suggesting that the information be placed in the specific employee's employment file.

Many say they have nothing to sue over. This is never true if the group is diligent in collecting information about the offending agency. Bureaucrats have complex rules that even they are never sure about, under which they must operate. More often than you'd guess there are rules that contradict other rules, so that whatever they do can be shown to violate the rules! They know all this and, if they believe that you know it too, they will be frozen into inactivity for fear that they will make procedural errors.

Fellow workers in the agency who similarly fear for their livelihood will pressure for additional discretion when dealing with this particular Political Action Group. Even the IRS, for instance, has modified its intransigent position a bit simply because citizens questioned its operating budgets the last few years.

One of the most common, favorite, and most effective avoidance techniques used by agencies to escape the planned wrath of freedom fighters is to try to shift the blame for problems to Somebody Else. In this one regard, bureaucrats can be amazingly clever. They may blame the city council, the legislature, state law or another agency. It takes a knowledgeable, alert political operative, backed by a committed brain trust, to escape this trap. Otherwise one is pushed into a dog-chasing-its-own-tail syndrome.

The bureaucracy does not have very many effective defenses other than the ploys of trying to shift blame and of hiding behind its rules. Bureaucrats really believe that if they do not hang together they will surely hang separately. The IRS even goes to the extreme of planning virtually all of its social activities collectively. Only members of the group are included. Somebody should picket one of its picnics to see the reaction of other citizens in the park, but be prepared to endure a three-day team tax audit if you try.

Pickets carrying signs listing specific names of bureaucrats along with suggestions about their duties, how much they make and where they live have an incredible impact even if the real issues are too difficult to articulate on the street.

Every time a conversation of any kind is held with an agency person, get the complete name. To some extent this will alleviate the all too common problem of being passed off from one person to another. Take pains to get secretaries' and receptionists' names. If someone does specialized work such as computer analysis or record retrieval, get these names as well.

It is also extremely helpful to do a short contact report on every person after every conversation. Admittedly these can become terribly tedious, but having the who, what, where, why and when six months into a particularly bloody campaign can be absolutely invaluable.

Letters sent to the agency should be copied for distribution to agency chiefs, media people, legislators. Include it in the group's newsletter. Vigorous distribution of blind copies really keeps the bureaucracy on edge while keeping the group alert to the public relations angles of every communication.

Freedom fighters should plan to pace their efforts against an offending agency so as to escalate efforts against it one step at a time. Always give the group a chance to consolidate gains while capitalizing on the rule that the threat of action is often worse than the action itself.

Chapter 28

Bureaucrats at Work

Without a doubt one of the best ways to get to know bureaucrats is to engage in open political warfare with them. Testing a person's political acumen and resolve is best done under stressful circumstances. However, if we wait till the day of battle, it will probably be too late. A successful political operative locked in battle with the bureaucracy must know the enemy's weak points well before combat gets serious. Initial strategies and their resulting tactics must take these weaknesses into account. There is no sense in setting the cannons banging away until you have a target to aim at.

One little recognized plus in this effort to learn about the enemy is that it occasionally gives us a chance to meet and use other bureaucrats who can actually help. Not all government bureaucrats are arrogant despots. Some are God-fearing, gentle souls who want nothing more than to continue with their relatively innocuous paper shuffling in obscurity. Some of these people can and will help the group, however timidly.

Be warned, though, that finding relatively decent bureaucrats can cause the group to falter in its resolve. It may be difficult to convince the troops that reaching the objective will require that a nice bureaucrat be socially, intellectually and vocationally destroyed. This is the downside to sending out the spies and a rule of political action that is distasteful to many. Yet there is no room to debate the merits of the situation. Whatever must be done must be done so that the greater good can be achieved and the group's lost freedom restored.

Always be sure to attack personal targets. In political warfare one cannot attack inanimate objects. Targets must never be general or abstract. School districts, police departments, planning and zoning commissions, the EPA, etc., are all examples of non-personal, inanimate objects. Freedom fighters who join battle with the like of these will waste the group's time and resources. Instead, attack the agency director or administrator by name.

Going after real people in the bureaucracy requires that one know these people, their wants, needs, hopes, beliefs, goals and aversions. Mere assumptions about government employees, however valid in general, should not take the place of focused intelligence gathering. This activity leads to an outside chance that the group may fall into the trap of admitting their opponent has some valid arguments or some intrinsic good. You can't let this idiocy happen or it will invariably lead to disharmony and contention within one's own community.

One of the best methods of getting to know opposition targets is to sit down and talk with them. And do it early! Obviously this must be done before the situation is polarized, before you tip your hand.

This often leads to a calculated formula approach to any new political project. On any new project make it a point to have breakfast every day with supporters and/or the brain trust and volunteers. Freedom fighters seem to enjoy this and you'll find that turnout is excellent. For lunch try as much as is humanly possible to schedule meetings with people who might be among your targeted bureaucrats. At the worst they may have no information, good or bad. When done early, they will readily sit down with a person picking up the tab. Their natural tendency will be to try to get you to "be reasonable," justifying their positions, citing rulings and trying to be philosophical. This is only human nature.

At these luncheon meetings ask unending questions about everything under the sun except the situation you know you are concerned about. Bureaucrats are human—when they're off duty! They very much enjoy talking about themselves. Ask where they went to school, where they live, how long they lived there, where they grew up, what their father did for a living. Ask about their interests, hobbies, the cars they drive, where their kids go to school, their general employment history, how much they like their current job, where they would like to go from here, where their wife (husband) works, ambitions for their children, and anything else you can think of. Like any good reporter, try to limit the conversation to talk about the other person. At the conclusion of the luncheon immediately transcribe your notes, listing as much detail as possible.

In addition, it is often effective to ask the brain trust to put the word out to find out if anyone among your group knows the bureaucrat's spouse, goes to church with them, or is in a club or group with them. These informal contacts, if they can be developed, yield mountains of good information. A drive past the bureaucrat's home noting name and model of vehicles, boats and campers can be informative.

Most bureaucracies have directories where one can obtain title, position, office and phone number. These directories are not commonly available, but whenever we needed one, by working a bit we usually managed to find one. Sometimes just by asking at the reception desk.

Knowing the bureaucrat's salary vis-à-vis the average for the area can be a tremendously useful piece of information. Finding out the GS rating, assuming federal employment, can be done simply by calling the bureaucrat's office and asking. Any government office or official can cite the salary range for a given rating. Ask the local army recruiter whenever you need current GS rating information. Until you do it, you can hardly appreciate the delicious public relations impact of exposing the high pay of a bureaucrat who is arbitrarily coming down on a group of relatively poor private-school teachers or small business people.

Knowing a bit about one's opponent allows the organization to orchestrate its tactics. It is important that the strategy be developed loosely enough to adapt to changing circumstances. When you give your target a good shove, or just get in a lucky hit, the bureaucratic reaction will provide the greatest source of aid and comfort to the Political Action Group, and point to new targets in the bargain.

Should you learn that an individual is in line for a fairly immediate transfer, try to work that fact into the strategy. If he is financially overextended and desperately in need of his current income, start looking for the agency employment policy to ascertain how fearful the bureaucrat might be of being frozen in his current position. If others in his family recently moved to the community to be near the bureaucrat, implementation of a Moose Jaw strategy (that is, the threat of a transfer to some miserable faraway post) may be appropriate.

These rules are effective guidelines:

1. Attack an individual and not a vague institution.
2. The attack is most effective when done on the basis of personal information about that individual's hopes, fears and weaknesses.
3. Good information about bureaucrats is much easier to collect early in the campaign.
4. The attacker should be cautious regarding any desirable characteristics of the antagonist. Occasionally it is tough to make out one's opponent as being totally evil.
5. Reactions to being attacked will vary, often providing the group with its next best point of attack. Those who come to the rescue of the bureaucracy are lumped together for similar treatment.
6. Fabricating an effective attack is arduous work, requiring the efforts of the best strategy-type people available to the group.
7. When gathering information, go first to the obvious sources, then be innovative about looking in every nook and cranny for additional details.

Chapter 29

Agency Rules and How to Fight Them

The word *bureaucracy* means "rule by bureau." Unfortunate but true, we are ruled by bureaus. Most of our laws are actually rules and regulations promulgated by state and federal agencies. For instance, it was a National Park Service rule, not any law passed by the Congress, that allowed the Yellowstone forests to burn down a few years ago. It is agency rules that turned lawnmowers into nearly unusable contraptions, that made pill bottles impossible to open, and that put those ridiculous little tags on mattresses and pillows.

Bureaus spin out unimaginable numbers of rules, measured in thousands of pages of fine print every year. Federal rule-making currently fills upward of 80,000 pages per year—something like all the phone books from every city in the country bound in one volume, all of it freedom-stealing rules with the force of law. Congress creates the bureaus; the bureaus themselves create the webs of regulation that grow into bureaucratic enslavement.

Naive, idealistic activists think that if only they can get their pet reform passed by Congress, it will solve some problem. What they actually get, every time, is a law that creates a new bureau. The baby bureau is soon writing rules and growing into a monster.

The idealists suppose the bureau will serve the public good. In fact, its primary interest is self-interest. A bureau is not elected so not accountable to the electorate. It doesn't have to please customers; it gets its money from taxes, license fees and fines that the customer can do little about. Agencies, in a word, are like little governments inside the bigger federal (or state) government. All but the smallest exercise legislative, executive, and judicial functions, and even have their own police forces (the "enforcement" or "compliance" branch). Like any other government, their tendency (as Jefferson observed) is to grow. The agencies write rules and more rules in order to grow and increase their own power.

Freedom fighters have to learn to contend with this reality and the arrogant mentality that it breeds.

To some extent legislators, assisted by concerned, freedom-fighting citizens, can work to rein in the bureaucracy. Agency budgets can be cut, destroying the agency's ability to expand or even maintain current levels of operations. More freedom-loving directors can be sought out and promoted as agency heads. We can use the Freedom of Information Act to harass bureaucrats and we can go to court more often to seek relief.

Admittedly, though, the selection of tools available to us is often meager. The bureaucratic tools used against us are convoluted and complex—which is actually an advantage for us. Knowing the system allows one to practice a sort of jujitsu and turn the bureaucracy against offending bureaucrats. This is one of the easiest means of prevailing against them.

Administrative agencies perform quite a number of different, often bewildering, duties. On the state and national level these are the agencies that most often impinge on individual freedoms in the course of making rules, or when they determine the cases or issues over which they supposedly have authority. Just having the authority to issue licenses, for instance, gives many of them tremendous power.

As recently as fifteen years ago, our principal concern was with federal agencies and their rule-making powers. Now the feds have mandated extensive new powers to the state to regulate pesticides, nuclear waste, asbestos and other things. Most of the states, with the feds as tutors, have taken up regulation. They, in turn, are acting as guides for local units of government in the areas of planning and zoning, parks and recreation, solid waste management, wastewater treatment and the like. For this reason, our battle is often with local commissions, which blame the state, which in turn blames the feds. Although this chapter concerns itself primarily with federal and state rule-making and enforcement, users should be prepared to apply many of the principles to the local level as well.

State administrative procedures acts are less formal than their federal counterpart, providing for additional citizen input on proposed rules both before and (at a stipulated time) after implementation. In some states, bad rules can sometimes be cut down after implementation. Opponents of regulations should make inquiry among legislators and/or attorneys regarding the procedures to follow. When public outcry is great, final approval may well be withheld.

The Freedom of Information Act should not be overlooked as an antibureaucratic weapon. Because of the importance of the amended FOIA, a separate chapter is dedicated to it alone. Another opening for freedom fighters lies in provisions of the Administrative Procedures Act that advance notice must be given before the agency can formulate a rule or decide a case. The act also provides that affected individuals must be given a hearing.

Rules that will be written by an agency in accordance with federal law must be published in the Federal Register. Given the explosive growth in this function of our government, the daily Federal Register has increased in size to the point where it is virtually impossible to pick out important individual items. In part this explains the dramatic growth in Washington, D.C., of associations ranging from everything from the National Rice Millers Association to the National Parking Association. Local groups find it is invaluable to associate with like-minded groups in Washington that will handle the detailed, time-consuming chore of reading the Federal Register in search of pertinent data for them. Special reading services have even sprung up whereby businesses that might be affected by items published in the Federal Register can hire people to watch for specified items.

This publication requirement gives groups of freedom fighters the right to find out about and comment on rules before they are finalized. It does *not* require that the agency listen to what is said or in any way incorporate the suggestions it receives into its final rules. In other words, offering testimony or comment is absolutely no guarantee that anything will be done. It is up to us to orchestrate pressure so that our recommendations will be considered.

As a rule, input must be made in writing. Usually agency rules require that comments submitted be summarized by the agency itself and published along with the final rule. In this regard, submitters do have input that becomes part of the published record. However, some agencies do not follow this procedure.

Often the real despotic power of an agency lies in its ability to issue licenses, set rates and to intercede in the development of private contracts. In times past, licensing restrictions impinged most broadly on the like of radio and TV broadcasters, aircraft manufacturers, public utilities and others who operate with what was said to be a "public monopoly." Today expect to be burdened with extensive licensing requirements for everything from selling firearms to manufacturing recreational vehicles, lawnmowers and concrete.

Bureaucrats and agency heads often hide behind the excuse that Congress has mandated the regulations they espouse. If one will look into the background of the enabling legislation it will be obvious that Congress did not have the specific actions in mind that the bureaucrats are pushing. This gives freedom fighters a point to attack. Good research can carry the day.

The Freedom of Information Act can be used to discover if enforcement is spotty and uneven. In most cases one will discover wide discrepancies in how the rules are applied. This gives you an opening to demand redress.

When dealing with administrative agencies, remember that our Constitution guarantees that no one can be deprived of life, liberty or property without due process of law. All other sources of law must meet this criterion. All agencies—national, state and local— have procedures that must be followed specifying rights of "aggrieved persons." It may be tough to uncover, but all agencies have due process by which they operate. This is their weak point. It is incumbent on us to uncover it.

Failing to operate "by the book" can embroil the agency in court actions that have the potential for horrible public relations and possible restraints on its actions. No bureaucrat in his right mind ever wants to rock the boat that much. Searching for an agency's unreasonable or arbitrary decisions and using them against it is one of the better new tactics available to aggressive Political Action Groups.

All of this dictates that PAG input into the rule-making proceedings be done earlier and more often than in the past. We simply must form more small, special interest groups sooner. Willingness to act quickly will, if nothing else, tend to overcome the problem of the agency chief who promulgates his or her narrow view of agency philosophy when writing rules.

As with most areas of politics, the agency administrators must really believe you will go to the wall with them, that you will fight them tooth and nail, both in courts of law and in the court of public opinion. Otherwise they will shrug off the attacks.

In summary, by law the agencies must follow their own set of procedures, the procedures must involve due process, and due process must include the opportunity for input from citizens like us. Making the agency do this can be done by smart, motivated citizens without legal training. The fight can be costly and difficult, leading through swamps full of bureaucratic alligators. But that's the price you have to pay, because of permanent bureaucratic powers dating back to the 1930s. Now there is no recourse except to work within the system in order to tie its hands.

Chapter 30

Freedom of Information Act

From the late 1960s, when the Freedom of Information Act was first passed by Congress, until the early 1970s when it was strengthened by amendment, a tremendous amount of information was published on the measure. Ralph Nader, the American Civil Liberties Union and even the Government Printing Office put out publications explaining in depth how one might go about using the Freedom of Information Act. Lately, however, the whole issue of forcing the bureaucracy to provide information seems to have fallen into the proverbial black hole. No one these days is talking very much about using this tool.

This is unfortunate since excellent opportunities still abound to use the act to fish for information about an agency, find out why it is acting as it is, gather potentially damaging data with which to wage war against it, and, most importantly, throw a monkey wrench into otherwise smooth bureaucratic operations. The power of using the act to delay and disrupt the bureau should be better known. The average bureaucrat is thrown very much off stride if operations do not run predictably and smoothly. Delays resulting from FOIA use can be anathema to the bureaucrats.

The Freedom of Information Act should not be confused with its half brother, the Privacy Act. Passed in 1974, the Privacy Act was originally designed to give citizens some control—and to some extent, say—over information collected and filed about them by the federal government. One of the principal provisions was to set in place a device that would allow average citizens access to data collected in their FBI or CIA files. The act prohibits these agencies from maintaining information contrary to freedoms guaranteed by the First Amendment.

Since the Privacy Act was principally designed to control federal information-gathering on citizens, most of its provisions relate to searching current files for personal information, reviewing them for accuracy and providing a means by which these files can be updated, purged and made more accurate. State equivalents to the Privacy Act are scarce to nonexistent.

The Freedom of Information Act, on the other hand, can peek into the bureau's own files and thus provide valuable information regarding how rules were promulgated, who protested, who directed that a thing be done, how others in similar circumstances were treated, the disposition of past cases, why specific cases were pursued, and more. Factual evidence may be gathered by this means that would be of use when challenging the regulations, suing the bureaucracy, creating work for bureaucrats, or just knowing to what extent the group can safely indulge in harassment or foot dragging.

Any Political Action Group doing battle with the federal bureaucracy or states with an Administrative Procedures Act ought to make early, liberal and ceaseless use of Freedom of Information requests. Since the public, press and even the government itself expects delays in the process and believes requests for additional information are not unreasonable, Freedom of Information actions can be made into a public relations plus if the group approaches them from this direction. Use FOIA requests as a subject of news conferences and news releases, mention them in newsletters and as an excuse for further delays when Big Brother says Act Now.

Keep in mind, however, that federal agencies would rather eat barbed wire than give out information they consider to be private, or to have their routine disrupted with FOIA requests. They will try a whole bag of standard tricks to avoid compliance. The degree to which it will cooperate is related to the philosophical underpinning of the agency chief, the agency policy, and the political clout and bias of the requesting group. When the group is believable, serious about the request, and has both the means and determination to go all the way into court, it has the battle half won.

Federal bureau chiefs will sternly and resolutely deny the truth of this contention, but in real life this is the way things work. The Sierra Club and Ralph Nader's groups, for instance, seem to have little problem acquiring all the information they desire under the FOIA because the bureau chief is sympathetic with their objectives.

Perhaps the best up-to-date contact one can use regarding Freedom of Information issues is the Freedom of Information Center, Box 858, Columbia, Missouri 65205. This office is a treasure chest of up-to-the-minute information on the subject of cracking into the bureaucracies' files. It maintains a sizable collection of materials pertaining to past agency decisions to release or not release information. The center will report in layman's terms on what has transpired for it shuns being regarded as a cold, hard repository of legal opinion.

One of the greatest services of the Freedom of Information Center is its ability to track state Freedom of Information laws and issues. Given the fact that there are fifty fast-changing state situations, this information on the bureaucracy is invaluable. In absolute *emergencies,* the center can be called at (314) 882-4856, but please do not tie up its phones and staff when your request is not critical.

The Freedom of Information Act dictates that every federal agency publish procedures for obtaining its files. Each agency has slightly different sets of rules and requirements. Often it hides behind these slight differences in the manner in which requests must be made when it wishes not to open its files. In this case, it is imperative that you determine the exact requirements for each agency. Then hound it till the desired results are achieved. Detailed agency FOIA regulations are available in the Code of Federal Regulations under the agency's official name and are commonly available at most city libraries, law offices and regional congressional offices.

The first step, when applying for information under the FOIA, is to know exactly and specifically which information is needed. This is never easy unless one has been regularly working with the agency regulating the problem at hand. The law, in this case, is plainly on the side of the agencies. It states that one must be able to describe the records sought reasonably and plainly.

Start early, expecting stonewalling when the bureaucrats don't want to make the records available.

The law allows for nine major areas of exemption wherein agencies are not required to release files. (The last two are special interest cases of scant use to us, so not reported below.) As a practical matter, unless the targeted agency is sympathetic, it always seems able to find some area of the code with which it can deny FOIA requests. The exclusionary areas are:

1. Documents classified as Secret or Classified. At the time a request is made, the agency must review its Secret classification for current validity, adjusting its documents accordingly.

2. Information memos and policies related solely to internal rules, policy and regulations. These include cafeteria policy, smoking and nonsmoking areas, parking lot rules, work rules and leave policy. These are usually not important unless one simply wants to embarrass the agency by publicizing its stupid rules.

   Staff policy manuals of guidelines for inspections for agents performing their duties are specifically not exempted under this section. These manuals can be a mine of good information, and the group should try to get one early in the game. On the other hand, agencies that have absolutely refused to release manuals have gotten away with it. The IRS, for instance, has traditionally refused to hand over copies of its audit criteria to inquiring citizens. In spite of over three years of litigation, including court decisions in favor of the plaintiff, the requested manuals have never been released.

3. Documents held by the Internal Revenue Service and Social Security Administration that are personal in nature, such as tax returns, medical and retirement records, census forms.

   Expert FOIA users say that files sought often end up mixed in this category, and that getting these files released is very difficult. Bureaus have their tricks.

4. Trade secrets and/or commercial financial information. However, companies having proprietary information they do not want released should not count on this portion of the act to protect them.

5. Personal/medical/employment files which, if disclosed, would clearly constitute an unwarranted invasion of privacy. On the face of it, this seems to be an overly broad category. However,

the trick word is "unwarranted." If a plausible explanation is included with the request, the intrusion could easily be found to be other than unwarranted. Requests in this area are often granted if they are carefully done.

6. Interagency or intra-agency memos. These are the documents that are often of greatest value. They can flag the extent to which an agency will most likely pursue a policy, who developed it and, often, why the policy is being pursued. Given the importance of this information, it is no coincidence that the agencies push as much material as possible into this file category.

   Innovation, persistence and past experience are needed to break through this defense. The Freedom of Information Center in Columbia, Missouri, will work with neophytes while they learn the nuances of the trade.

7. Law enforcement and investigatory procedures. This information supposedly can be held by the agencies if they believe it falls within their law enforcement activities and duties.

Several fairly hot court cases have been adjudicated in this last area. The courts have held that this type of information must be released unless there is imminent prospect of law enforcement or potential interference with enforcement proceedings. If disclosure might deprive a person of a fair trial or reveal the identity of a confidential source, the information can be withheld.

Stonewalling and Delays

Since delay is often used as a tactic by offending agencies, when making a FOIA request, stipulate a time frame in which the agency should reply. Suggest that it at least acknowledge your request in seven to ten working days. Coupled with a specific and detailed request for documents, your suggestion puts a great deal of pressure on the agency to respond. If it does not respond, it may be necessary to go to your senator, representative or attorney as a means of applying additional pressure. At times a relatively simple letter requesting clarification on the matter from one of them will do the trick.

In all cases, ask the agency to substantiate statutorily any denials or delays. All documents related to the matter should be carefully retained for possible future use.

The following are among the most common ploys agencies use to duck FOIA requests. They are listed in order of frequency of use by agencies:

1. Claiming that the material is part of internal communications as set out in exemption 6 of the code.

   It is tough to beat this because you must prove both that the communication exists and that it is "material to policy" and of genuine interest to the group.
2. Exemptions claimed for information to be used in enforcement.

   This is more and more common, as various agencies take up the role of policeman in our overregulated society. (See item 7 of the statutory exclusions.)
3. Exemptions claimed for personal information given in confidence. This is exemption 5, which often seems to be stretched past the breaking point by bureaucrats.
4. Claiming the file is empty. Unless one can persuade a judge that it makes no sense for the file to be empty—not easy to do—this ploy can too often defeat FOIA requests.
5. Agencies will often mix information that is clearly exempt from release with other nonexempt data so as to preclude outsiders from acquiring useful information in an entire file.
6. An often-used, relatively successful tactic is to delay the release process in the hope that the inquirer will lose interest or run out of money waiting. Court cases support the inquirer, but these actions are sometimes costly to initiate and litigate.
7. Some agencies use the tactic of assessing exorbitant charges for copying documents. Statutory provisions set out costs that can be assessed for searching through files, but agencies have in the past tried to assess twenty-five cents a page, or more, for copies. In many cases the requested files may have hundreds of superfluous pages of no direct relation to the issue at hand, for which the bureaucrat will expect payment.

If the agency persists in stonewalling, the federal act specifically says, "The district court of the United States in the district in which the complainant resides, or has his principal place of business, or in which the agency records are situated, has jurisdiction to enjoin the agency from withholding agency records and to order the production of any agency records improperly withheld from the complainant" [5 USC 552 (a) (3)].

This means that if the bureaucrats turn down the Political Action Group, the latter can go to court in its own district without going to Washington, D.C. Freedom of Information Act time is hardball time. Start as early as possible on the process. When the group needs help, do not hesitate to call upon the Freedom of Information Center in Missouri. Another helpful group is the Freedom of Information Clearing House, Box 19367, Washington, D.C. 20036. These people are also used to providing expert guidance to nonspecialists who want to negotiate the Freedom of Information swamp.

Sample Request Letter
Freedom of Information Act

(Name) Public Information Officer

_____Agency

(Address)

Dear _____:

Pursuant to the Freedom of Information Act, 5 USC 552, and to the regulations of (name of agency or department), CDR (citation to departmental regulations, obtainable from committee print index), I hereby request access to (records desired, identify with as much detail as can be provided).

If there is a charge for locating and copying the requested material, please notify me in advance of the estimated amount.

Please reply to this request by (date, allowing the agency reasonable time to process the request, usually seven to ten days). If the request is denied, please specify the section of the Freedom of Information Act which is being relied on as legal basis for the denial.

Thank you for prompt attention to this request.

Sincerely,

_____

Chapter 31

Using One Bureaucracy Against Another

Our crew was absolutely furious.

Linda, the community activist gadfly, had used our own office information, which we openly provided, to create three days of extra work for our busy staff. She outfoxed and outmaneuvered us to the point that it would have been truly serious had we not been scrupulously careful with all our processes up to that point. As it was, we simply had egg all over our faces. The office staff assumed that by being nice to a known opponent and demonstrating that we were both careful and serious, we might win her over. The staffers were new to politics, unprepared for what happens when all-out political war is declared. They got quite a lesson.

The incident started when a group of businessmen, for whom author Grupp set up a project, got together in their economically struggling community to encourage new business. We established a local development corporation and sold shares of stock, using the proceeds to buy a piece of land on which we intended to locate new job-intense manufacturers.

Linda represented a small but previously effective group of community obstructionists who remained adamantly opposed to any new developments. They were No-Growthers, with a vengeance. They were also smart—but unused to duking it out with anyone with previous experience.

Linda stopped by the development office, using some of her inexhaustible supply of time, to chat with the office staff about what was going on. Since everything we did was public as well as approved by the secretary of state, it did not seem appropriate to play games. We gave her whatever information she requested. In retrospect we believe we basically did the correct thing. But we ended up making it easier for her to audit us.

She took down the names of all the original incorporators and major stockholders, and took copies of the corporate statement of policy, articles of incorporation and minutes of the meetings so far. Armed with these, she went to her supporters to wave a red flag and raise money. From there she stopped at her attorney's office and he reviewed the documents for correctness. She took the documents to the state attorney general's office to determine if we could legally sell stock under current state law for the purpose for which we said we existed. At the secretary of state's office she confirmed that we had crossed every T and signed every blank so that no opportunity existed to involuntarily dissolve the corporation or accuse it of fraud. She checked our office lease at the courthouse, checked with the state regarding our workers compensation, inquired about our business license, state tax number, age of our employees, hours, pay rate, health department requirements and on and on.

Every stop she made produced telephone requests to us for more information from the bureaucracy, using considerable amounts of staff energy at a time when time was very much at a premium. We were in the thick of battle. Each needless interruption seemed especially maddening.

It was our bad luck, too, that a scam involving sales of stock for a golf course had recently embarrassed several key officials. Each called, asking us to hold up on our activities till he could send an aide up to check firsthand. The deputies who looked us over found nothing irregular, and allowed us to continue, but only after two days of delay.

Despite some tense moments, the aggravation and the embarrassment of knowing we had been outfoxed, everything worked out okay. Linda demonstrated that the state bureaucracy she knew so intimately could be used to fight the business she hated.

As a reward for Linda's attentions we placed her house on the National Historic Register. Registration effectively stopped her from doing any major renovation in her own house for fear she could not sell to anyone using government-secured financing. Perhaps this can no longer be done without the owner's consent, but at the time it could.

We did it.

The incident, if nothing else, alerted us to the need to review all of one's options and to find out if other bureaucracies can be of assistance when dealing with an obstreperous bureaucracy one's PAG has targeted or an opposed political action committee.

Going to the state attorney general is the obvious first step. The AG can advise on state freedom of information possibilities, on state and federal constitutional questions and, to a great extent, on state and local bureaucratic procedural issues.

More than a few state attorneys general will also take on the feds if they believe the situation has the potential to give them long-term, positive political exposure. Certainly in a fight with the federal bureaucracy, it does no harm to ask. Your group, in return, implicitly offers political support that should be welcome. A startling number of our sitting governors have come up through the ranks, starting as attorneys general. Semipermanent groups should stay close to their state attorneys general. It is up to the individual group whether to raise money, include statements in its newsletters, provide mailing lists, distribute yard signs and even do some direct campaigning for the candidate if it seems appropriate.

At times, state attorneys general will only issue opinions on local, state and federal rules in response to requests from elected officials. In most cases this is not a problem. Local legislators will generally do about anything for constituents that they feel will not obviously cost them votes. Requesting information in behalf of a group of activists is usually neither costly nor risky, politically. Legislators often cooperate, provided the group is willing to do the rough draft of the letter for them.

The greatest ally we have when fighting the feds is the federal Freedom of Information Act. Use of the act as part of an integrated, thoughtful strategy can cause bureaucrats an incredible amount of trauma and labor. (See chapter 30.)

Other than special situations such as going to one's attorney general, or the use of a specific act such as the FOIA, be warned, you will walk a very thin line when going to the enemy for aid and comfort. Even if it is another seeming friendly portion of the camp one is dealing with, it is still the enemy's camp.

Bureaucracies as a rule would rather add additional rules, procedures and regulations than trust the judgment of citizens. It is a manifestation of their "wisdom" that government is always smarter than the citizens. We all know this is ridiculous, but it is an untruth with which we must continually contend. In every case, the bureaucracy only asks that you give up only a minor amount of freedom in exchange for making its work-related routine go more smoothly. Those who elect to walk this hair-thin line between freedom and government control must evaluate every move in these terms. Alert activists will very likely uncover several agencies that might be drawn into offering assistance. Before accepting any such aid, one must ask what the cooperating agency will ask in return. Also, evaluate from every possible angle how an offending agency's routine might be disturbed by another agency, so that you won't face surprises and stay in charge if you act.

The following suggestions are not really rules. They may do little more than sensitize the reader to the possibilities of maneuvering one branch of government against another.

The easiest actions are on the local level. Personalities enter into the picture the most here, and the group can play on these to pit one branch of government against another. Local units of government often don't know what they are doing anyway, lacking the expertise it takes to stay out of trouble that freedom fighters might drag them into. At times the state can be coerced into taking the part of local citizens against the feds. On the national level, odd things happen if one is just clever enough to root them out.

Activists should not overlook the possibility that their local planning and zoning commission might help by not zoning, zoning to something else, or deciding that a proposed use is impossible. Admittedly this is a remarkably close approximation to playing with skunks. Our mothers warned us how we'd smell after doing that, so exercise caution and draw on the wisdom and counsel of the brain trust.

Until a few years ago the federal government was happy to lead the charge against private property rights, notwithstanding that they are constitutionally protected. Cities, states and the feds themselves used regulation, zoning, delays and other devices to take citizens' property without compensation. Due process, in many cases, amounted to little more than confiscation by formula.

Happily, those days are gone forever, according to recent Supreme Court rulings. In March 1988 President Reagan issued an executive order to all agencies that set out tough new guidelines related to taking property by zoning. The executive order was written by the Justice Department. The guidelines were prompted, in part, by claims of owners for over $1 billion in damages as a result of these "takings" that the Supreme Court determined to be illegal. Most of the claims were against the Environmental Protection Agency.

As part of the order, agencies must do a "taking implication analysis" before federal regulators do anything to affect private property and thereby risk undue additional exposure to additional lawsuits. The group should check on this and may well find an avenue for action. A fellow political activist has sued several environmentalists personally after they held up a shopping center for eight years. He believes that, to the extent the individuals have assets, he will recover. At least the opponents will spend most of their own—and perhaps their group's—funds defending themselves in court for the next few years. If more of us did this, we could rout those who infringe our inalienable rights.

Many freedom issues can be couched in terms of the taking of civil rights or discrimination. If there appears to be some way the group can make this claim, do so through the U.S. Commissioner on Civil Rights, Washington, D.C., or at eight regional commissions around the country. Plausible civil rights complaints can cause an agency no end of grief, and perhaps divert it from other actions against the group for a time too.

On all three levels of government it is often effective to go to competing agencies suggesting that the group will lead an attack on an offending agency's budget to the benefit of the competitor if they will provide deep background information and informal help.

Using one agency in this manner against another is often best left in the hands of an experienced political operative. Unlike many other aspects of this business, it is not easy to predict how and when it will work properly.

Chapter 32

Factoids and Other Political Agents

A *factoid* is a half-truth, unproven theory, wild exaggeration or flat lie posing as scientific fact. Many have never heard of one, yet there are scads of them flying around. Factoids, indeed, are one of the most pervasive and despicable political devices in common use today. Their context is virtually always political and individually they are always difficult to deal with. Our Side had better be warned and ready.

Factoids are a relatively recent phenomenon. They exploit the layman's ignorance of advanced technology, academic theory, policy or science—and who among us, except the specialist, knows much about these things? It is hard to pin an exact definition on factoids because they come in so many shapes and sizes. But by definition all factoids include elements of massive exaggeration. They are structured to mislead in technical areas that are difficult or impossible to document. Factoids play on our fears or suspicions, facing us with some Terrible Threat that we cannot refute.

Factoids in use are always quick little items that the media can easily pick up and use over and over again. Combating them is tough.

For instance:

- Pesticides applied by farmers are contaminating millions of wells, causing thousands to die of cancer annually.
- PCBs cause cancer.

- Enacting this new asbestos bill will save thousands of lives annually.
- Thousands of children will grow up illiterate and socially crippled as the result of a home school education.
- Any level of radiation is harmful.
- Children attending a school located near a power transmission line suffer learning disabilities.

In the search for the biggest and best factoid, we submit the statement made by Dr. Ernest Sternglass back in 1969, published in *Penthouse* magazine, setting out that "all children in the U.S. would ultimately die from fallout caused by nuclear testing."

We have all heard thousands of factoids. People who suddenly become sensitized to look for factoids are amazed to realize that they are used carte blanche by the media. We are pummeled with them daily in our paper and on TV. When they are analyzed, they can easily be seen to be beliefs or claims without scientific evidence. Yet, after the factoids are repeated over and over, even reasonable, well educated people tend to go along with what is, in reality, a deliberate, massive deception, especially if no credible source vocally disputes them.

It is as if scientific questions common to our modern technological world were settled by debate, rather than empirical evidence. But this is absurd! A scientific fact is a fact whether the public believes it, or likes it, or not.

The disinformation of factoids becomes especially severe for those who must deal with public perception of social issues. Here the mix of science, values and experience is as explosive as a kid with matches in the gasworks. In the social sciences the problems dealing with factoids that probably never can be proved or disproved are epidemic. How does one argue against the statement that spending $13 million more on government medical care would save 90,000 babies' lives each year, for instance? For related reasons, factoids are often used in a personal health context, elevating their shrillness dramatically.

Use of factoids is virtually epidemic when discussing pesticides, asbestos, nuclear power, chemicals of any sort, education, military spending and ozone layer. We also often encounter them in battles over home schools, planning and zoning, national speed limits, opening a new business, public school bond issues, creationist vs. evolutionary theory, etc.

In conventional debate situations, it is always incumbent on the asserter to offer proof that the assertion is correct. In a public relations or political fracas, the side that thinks up the cleverest, most strident factoid nearly always wins. Opponents of technological or social change need only make a vaguely plausible, scientific-sounding charge that the change would bring a calamity. No matter how preposterous, the factoid will almost always be accepted as true if it is repeated often enough.

Offense is the best defense, so mount the counterattack immediately. Attack the credibility of those making the assertion. Attack from every angle: personnel, funding, scientific sources, membership, political motives, everything. If the disinformation spreaders aren't credible, they won't be believed.

Using or not using insupportable "facts" in one's battle against the bureaucracy is a judgment call that each Political Action Group must make for itself. Making this decision is not as easy as one would suppose. In the trenches during a pitched political battle, one's perspective can change.

Here are some considerations about the use of factoids:

1. Factoids will be used extensively against the group if it shows any sign of being successful.
2. There is virtually no defense against clever and insistently repeated factoids except, perhaps, counterfactoids. Once a factoid offense is evident against your group, begin your own attack on the Other Side's credibility, and do not stop.
3. Use of factoids is criminally easy and criminally effective. Even dull political strategists can usually dream up dozens of workable factoids.

Many of us take as an article of faith that the truth will always triumph over ignorance and error. It probably will some day, but in the meantime the false charge or error is scoring all the political points. The battle can easily be lost, and often is, before the truth has a chance to catch up. It is a mistake to think that Our Side or any honest political player can deal with factoids easily, by asserting the truth. As a practical matter there is no 100 percent effective method of handling them. Once the accusation is made, people tend to remember it, especially if it is catchy, short and plausible. We must accept the fact that, in our times, a basic untruth works on people's minds till they take it to be truth.

To a certain extent, defenders in battle with factoid users can challenge every one, every time a factoid is used. They must then get their own experts, who will offer solid evidence that the contention of the accusing group is ill founded. This can be a long, expensive and arduous task. It will require extensive, time-consuming research that really should be the duty of the asserters. The worst of it is that the group will continually find itself on the defensive. Campaigns are often lost that way.

On a state or national level there is no effective defense, only the most merciless offense directed against the opponent's credibility. As factoids are false, those who spread them are fair game for ad hominem arguments. Question their motives. Link them to one political party and to any plausible special interests. The media are relatively quick to sniff out and glom onto situations where players are feathering their own nest. Hollering "conflict of interest" neither addresses nor refutes the hostile factoids, but it does catch citizens' attention. Conflicts of interest occur at many levels and can virtually always be validly alleged.

Don't hesitate to call the Other Side's charge a factoid. Handle it with humor, avoiding the entire issue of truth or correctness, if possible. Continually request supporting facts and figures and, when they are not forthcoming, suggest that "what we are dealing with is another factoid without scientific or social merit, designed to dupe the public." It's a variation of Ronald Reagan's "there you go again" ploy used so effectively in the 1980s debates.

Factoids are such a problem in our political process that perhaps it is time to confront them as a phenomenon. A group might reap great benefit for the community by challenging factoids wherever they are found, whether they are political or not.

Chapter 33

Dress to Win

Politics and its kissin' cousin, public relations, are packed to overflowing with non-verbal communications and symbolism. It isn't always what the group says or does that counts. Many times the important factor is how it looks when it is doing it—a variation on the adage "it isn't whether you win or lose, but how you *look* when playing the game." It is essential that the group gets these nonverbal signs right if it expects everything else to fall into place. Group members can work smart and hard, but if their spokesmen and public followers do not "look right," they will not be received positively.

The first line of nonverbal communications is dress, haircut and good-looking shoes. As in many other areas of political action, a dress code has been carefully worked out. Proven, predictable formulas are available that will be effective virtually 100 percent of the time, projecting the image of honesty, competence, sincerity and credibility.

The problems with these formulas—precise and proven as they are—are that, first, we don't really believe that they are true, or that they will actually work; and second, the formulas contain very costly surprises.

Dressing correctly and credibly is costly. A suit purchased for Uncle Fred's funeral, for instance, or one worn to church regularly, may be entirely inappropriate for effective political actions. Moreover, the people to whom we traditionally turn to make the decisions regarding clothing should not (it turns out) be entrusted with this task. Most men, for instance, rely on their wives for help in picking out suits, dress shirts, ties and other business clothing.

Experts in political attire, however, tell us that women use a sub-liminal perception markedly different from the one needed to project credibility via clothing. (Don't get irked, ladies, we're just reporting! Besides, men still need your better taste in clothing for social or business purposes.)

Haircuts also fit into this syndrome. Credible political representatives have very short, recently trimmed hair. Many women, on the other hand, prefer men to have slightly longer hair. Women are looking for something different from what reporters want . . . we hope.

The area of image building got a tremendous boost about twenty years ago when John T. Malloy discovered that salesmen trying to get interviews with an executive were successful a far greater percentage of the time when they showed up at the front office wearing tan raincoats. The same actors who appeared at the reception desk wearing black or dark blue were perceived to be low-class individuals who did not warrant any favors. They were forced to wait much longer. Some never did get in to see the man they sought. This and other similar research ushered in the era of programmed, conservative dress for group spokesmen calculated to send sub-liminal messages putting one's colleagues and even competitors at ease. As a result, today few salesmen, politicians, lawyers, businessmen or bankers are unaware of the need to "dress for success."

Masters in the advertising business lavish care on evaluating the needs and expectations of those who are receiving ad messages. When making commercials they spare no pains finding people who look and dress like believable nurses, mechanics, farmers, attorneys, soap users, or any other consumer they want to portray. The point should be clear to activists that politics, too, requires careful dramatizations of just the same sort.

We can readily agree that if we expect our spokesmen to carry our side of an issue to supporters and voters, we must use people who project an image appropriate to the task. A person who looks like school teacher will be more effective explaining private school issues than will a fashion model, for instance. In talking about educating children, the svelte woman in an expensive designer dress with long black hair cannot compete for credibility with a silver-haired, well-groomed, slightly overweight, matronly woman dressed in a modest outfit. Even if the targeted group that one is trying to influence is composed of counterculture types, the spokesman with the teacher image will prevail. The counterculturists remember their own grade school days and from this and many other sources, have the same image of teachers as anyone else; their own dress is irrelevant.

Similarly, an executive in a black pinstripe suit and wing-tip shoes, for example, will find it nearly impossible to persuade a general audience that a proposed sewer line is economically and technically suitable, whereas the same executive might easily make the point dressed in tan work clothes, field boots, wearing a battered hard hat. Subliminal influences hinge on these sorts of deep, hidden signals.

In all our political endeavors, therefore, we need to pay more attention to the details of building credibility via dress and other aspects of our appearance. Happily, this is an area where we still have an edge over the slovenly, tennis-shoed, poorly dressed spokesmen who typically push environmentalist causes.

Politicians know that images are important. When out in cattle country they wear cowboy hats and western-cut suits. Down in mines, boots and slicker and head lamp are proper. When they go on national TV they always wear the obligatory dark suits, white shirts and solid, properly contrasting ties. Politicians of slight stature wear darker, more severe suits. Larger men attempt to soften their image and broaden their appeal by wearing somewhat lighter suits, usually soft plaids.

Some of the research findings are maddening to those who have never thought about the issue of one's dress and its relation to credibility. Although the original research was done to enable attorneys, businessmen and salesmen to be more effective, there is a wide application throughout our society. Businessmen should look like credible, successful businessmen. Politicians should project honesty, though most do so by sneaky means!

Rules of dress apply to anyone appearing before groups, media people, folks trying to raise money or even one's inner group of followers.

Although many people cannot articulate their inner feelings or even admit they are happening, subliminal signals sent out by the wearer tell them exactly what kind of a person they are dealing with. Is the person a liar? We will think so if an elderly person dresses like a twenty-five-year-old. Is a businessman competent? We might think not, if he dresses in polyester suits that are not tailored perfectly. Is anyone serious who wears a bow tie? People think that only clowns, restaurant waiters, college professors and very few others (Sen. Paul Simon) wear bow ties. Should anyone else do it, he'd probably be written off as a clown.

Experts who have spent huge amounts of effort studying the issue offer a few fairly straightforward rules regarding clothing that should be absolutely inviolable. Those who follow them will be perceived as being more believable and will receive preferential treatment.

Although most of the tactics of clothing were developed and tested for men, similar rules apply to women. However, our frame of reference is obviously male. Most of the people with whom we worked in front line PR roles were men. The professional women who come on the various boards already know the clothing rules, saving us the grief of researching the nuances of female "dress for success." Because it is more difficult for women executives to rise through the ranks, they are already going to be more keenly aware of the role dress plays by the time they assume a leadership role in political activities.

All clothing should be very, very conservative, always fitting in with contemporary standards of the community. This varies dramatically from community to community and, of course, with the group one is trying to influence. Because this is true, dressing properly can at times present a dilemma. When one must deal with the local media and electorate and then journey to Washington, D.C., to meet with senior agency bureaucrats, proper wardrobes get very tricky. Throw in a visit to a congressman's office and a second, somewhat different outfit may be required. In every case, dress exactly as the kind of person you wish to project.

In a business or political context, avoid flagging your socioeconomic class or background by your clothing. The goal should be to look very proper, well-turned-out, upper middle class. The only exception occurs when one purposely intends to build credibility as a doctor, scientist, teacher, lab technician or other technical person at hearings or in a media context. In this case, dress in a manner that might even be considered corny or affected. The object, in this case, is to look credible by looking the part.

Otherwise play it safe and dress "upper-middle-class prosperous." Do this by dressing conservatively and as expensively as possible (quality clothing wears better so the per-usage cost will not be prohibitive).

Starting at the top, always wear a well pressed, perfectly fitted white shirt. The shirt should never shine, and contain as much cotton and as little polyester as one can find to purchase. Shirts purchased off the shelf will not fit this well and must be turned over to a tailor for alterations.

Suits should be all wool or as low a percentage of polyester as possible. Pick high-quality fabrics that do not wrinkle easily. Fabrics can be tested by twisting a suit coat or a pant leg. High-priced, high-quality fabrics do not wrinkle easily. Subdued plaids, solid blues, lightly textured grays, gray flannels, beige and teal blue are all acceptable. Very dark to black suits are only acceptable on smaller men. Pants should always be cuffed.

The real trick when buying a proper suit is to get it fitted correctly. Some experts firmly believe that no suit purchased off the rack can ever be made to fit correctly. Talk in person to the tailor who will do the alterations; allowing the store clerk to pin up the suit is unacceptable. The tailor must be made to understand that the suit must fit perfectly and that doing extra fittings for extra payment is no problem. Wear the shoes that will be worn with the suit. Fill your pockets with all of the items normally carried when wearing a suit. Be sure the pants do not pull or wrinkle and that the suit coat fits without a wrinkle even after you have been sitting in a chair in the store.

Those uncertain of what they are doing are much safer in purchasing a well known, quality brand name suit such as Hart Shaffner and Marx, After Six, Brooks Brothers or others of similar quality.

Shoes should always be black, dark brown or cordovan. They may be wing tips or conventional conservative loafers, but must always be dressy looking and must be made of leather. Shoes must always be well polished. Many image builders recommend that one's shoes always be professionally polished.

Belts must match one's shoes. They must be put together with smaller, expensive buckles. The buckle should always be fairly plain. Ties are surprisingly important. The rule of thumb is to buy one twice as expensive as one can possibly afford. Always choose silk for one's ties. Pick solid, conservative colors, small polka dots, heavy stripes or conservative subdued paisleys. Backing and liners in the tie should be dense enough so that good, solid knots can be tied. Ties must complement one's suits in a conservative manner. Flashy loud prints are absolutely unacceptable.

Socks must be black and long enough to cover one's ankles and calves, even when one is sitting down. Polyester is acceptable for socks.

Do not wear tie clasps, rings other than wedding bands, or any other gaudy accessories. Cuff links are okay as long as they look expensive. Cheap or unconventional watches such as pilot's watches, driving watches or other such are a no-no. Wear the most expensive watch possible.

Unless it is your intention to be immediately branded, and lumped with a particular special interest group, avoid any social, fraternal, religious or political buttons, pins or ties. If they signal anything at all, they may detract from your overall message.

When purchasing clothing destined to be worn in a political/public relations context, be eternally wary of store clerks. Even senior, experienced men's store clerks have an entirely different agenda from yours. Their purpose is to move the merchandise they have on hand regardless of the buyer's real needs. Some items may go out of fashion, leaving the clerk with items that must be discounted to clear out of the store. Clearance items are seldom acceptable to the properly turned-out spokesman.

Never wear anything green, short-sleeved shirts or any item that might even remotely be considered effeminate. Sports jackets are never, ever permissible.

Three-piece suits are appropriate in some regions. The trick is to determine in which region they will be most effective.

When going to a new city, observe the mayor's clothing style. From there, go to talk to the bankers whose dress always reflects quiet, steady credibility in the community. If this still does not give a good idea regarding suits, ties and shoes, then watch the local TV station's late news to see what the male and female newscasters are wearing.

In sum, no one who is preparing to enter the political battle-ground should consider doing so without a proper uniform. Our people seem intuitively to know more about this process than do professional activists, though the enemy has finally begun to figure this out. We should continue to press our advantage and put the money and effort into mastering the process.

Chapter 34

Polling
(and other activities that look like polling)

P olling is, without a doubt, the single greatest operational tool available to the political/public relations activists. Polls are invaluable when working on initiatives or in head-to-head partisan conflicts. Some old-line local politicians may wish otherwise, but modern political warfare cannot be successfully waged without information provided by polls. The only exception might occur in a relatively small campaign using a brain trust.

More subtle than polling, and much more difficult to execute, is the mock poll. The mock-pollster elicits "information" by asking questions which sensitize polled individuals to an issue. Carefully phrased questions demonstrate to the polling target that he has not yet considered the matter carefully enough. Questions in this "poll" predispose the respondent either to support your position or to make unpalatable answers illustrating the weaknesses of the opponents' position.

Polling is much like baking cakes from a package mix. Once one has the package, the remainder is fairly straightforward. Some people are intuitively better than others at polling, yet there is a formula that will produce predictable results. Amateurs, when they must, can conduct good, solid information-producing polls. Smaller, local contests are especially subject to the edge polls provide.

Most of us are willing to work toward political objectives, but lack the experience and knowledge it takes to mount a successful

174

campaign. Local contests where money is limited are an especially puzzling problem. Polls cut right to the heart of the matter, giving us tools needed to mount an effective low-cost offensive. In most cases these little polls are quick and quite inexpensive. Smaller, local polls use the same basic assumptions as those done on a state and national basis.

In these times it is even unusual for people with telephones not to have been contacted by a poll taker. At times the concept is still poorly defined, but citizens have come to realize that polls provide a reasonably accurate picture of what is happening at the time it was taken. When people change their minds, new polls will reflect these changes by taking a new political photo.

If anything, people are growing weary of the many polls, especially those who do not like the results they see. Polling as a means of predicting trends is more accurate than it has ever been. Polls will continue to be useful, probably in smaller and smaller campaigns.

Among apolitical, average citizens, there is still only limited recognition that polls provide information as to what is on people's minds, how to handle issues and what significance if any they attach to a given issue. Citizens recognize that polls can predict how people vote, but do not seem to realize they also explain *why* they vote as they do. Political operatives who truly understand the differences between these concepts and are willing to use little polls in local contests have taken a quantum lead in the race to amass and orchestrate political power.

The main duty of polls is to define community perception regarding issues and perceptions. Professional pollsters do not care who is winning nearly as much as they care why. Proper polls tell us how people perceive issues. From that we learn how to package and develop those issues, how to talk about them, where to spend the group's money and, in general, how to prevail in a rough and tumble competitive atmosphere.

Development and interpretation of polls are admittedly tough, demanding operations. While it may be best to allow professionals to handle the group's polling if the money and professionals are available, it certainly is not a requirement. Political activists should not allow the absence of professional pollsters to become an excuse for not taking polls. The rule is always to use a brain trust and nearly always to use polls. This requirement seems to be overkill, but even tiny, obscure, completely local contests that look like walkaways can go down the tube because one did not take the time and trouble to see what was really going on.

In the pure and customary sense, when one actually wishes to sample populations in an attempt to predict the composition, fairly sophisticated statistical techniques must be employed. These techniques are based on the premises, proven by mathematical techniques and actual practice, that one need randomly sample only a small, representative portion of any large population to predict the characteristics of the entire population. Sampling overcomes the sheer mechanical problems of talking to everyone—who can call one hundred million voters in the U.S.? That just isn't feasible, but we *can* call a few thousand households and get an accurate picture of the whole.

The trick here is to find pollees who are truly representative of the entire population but selected randomly. In politics it isn't that easy. Regional variations come into play. Pollsters must blend the regional differences into the sample, being sure that the regional group is not given too much or too little weight in the whole population. Within a city, for example, if one section of the city comprises atypical, poorly educated, working-class people, but if they number only 3,000 of the total 100,000 in the city, it would be foolish to take more than 3 percent of one's sample from this group. Sophisticated national pollsters go to great lengths to be sure that their sample is representative.

Statisticians use complex formulas to determine how many people should be polled so that the correct number is included in the sample, yielding the degree of confidence one demands from the results. Average citizen groups with limited funds and perhaps limited statistical talent can look in a handbook of statistical tables under "sample size." These tables will tell them how many people to poll in order to achieve the needed degree of accuracy. Use of tables will produce excellent results but will cause the group to do a little extra work, calling more people than if they worked out the sample mathematically. This gives a more accurate result so is desirable anyway.

There is little problem in picking homogenous representatives to telephone in a local poll. In smaller towns, the socio-economic differences in the people tend not to be significant. Depending on the accuracy you need, you can just call every third, eighth or fifteenth name in the phone book, and not have to worry much that you are getting a good picture. Keep polling over your target number if you have any doubts.

If by some chance one particular group is overrepresented in the sample, results will be skewed and misleading. Work with the brain trust to keep this from happening. More problems arise in sampling larger, irregular populations. At times one may run into situations where large numbers of responders live one place and vote or pay taxes in another, are attached to a military base, are not eligible to vote, are students who are away at school during elections and so on. It is impossible to list all of the eventualities that might spoil a pollster's tidy little sample. They are out there. Beware and plan accordingly.

Having taken as many factors as possible into consideration, the pollster probably can simply take the appropriate phone book in hand, count the number of phones, divide by the size of the needed sample and start calling. For example, if there are 5,000 phones listed and 586 responses must be solicited, call every eighth line in the book. Instruct those calling on polls to mark every name they try. If there is no answer, then go to the next and then next again till a valid contact is made. It is best to call in the evening from 7:00 to 9:00, though like other factors this should be tested. Under some circumstances pollers may work during the day, attempting to pick up those they missed. When businesses are mixed in with residences in the phone book and the designated number falls on a business, go on to the next residence.

As a general rule use the number 435 in any samples for most of the smaller local initiative elections. Results have usually been satisfactory with no real surprises. On populations of half a million or more use a sample of 665.

At this writing, costs are usually as follow. Use volunteers if possible. If not, pay $1 per call to hire people to do the work. At a cost of $435 to $665 that is cheap access to a huge amount of information. In this case, the budget item is certain and easy to predict.

So far all of this is probably relatively straightforward even for people who are not enamored of mathematics. The real challenge is handling the social elements of the questionnaires if one chooses to go for the gold and ask more than "whom are you going to vote for?"

Because developing the questions for a poll and then interpreting them are so difficult, hire a pro if one is available. If not, don't despair; your brain trust can develop polls and get valid interpretations of the results. It will take a bit longer to do the experimenting needed to find the correct questions, but the results will eventually be there.

Now let's see how to do it in practical terms.

When writing polls, start with the obligatory "Good evening, I am taking a public opinion survey. Your name was selected at random and because your individual response is of value, we would like to know if you have a few minutes to answer questions."

Telephone interviewers should be coached to put down detailed quotes whenever possible, never inserting their own preconceived notions or wording. All interviews must be done from standard printed forms.

Be sure all of the rules are written out in detail for each of the callers:

Are you a registered voter? Yes ☐ No ☐

Do you know about the _____ initiative on which you will be asked to vote November 7? Yes ☐ No ☐

Do you generally vote in (bond, initiative, primary) elections? Yes ☐ No ☐

Do you generally vote Democrat or Republican, or do you always split your ballot? Democrat ☐ Republican ☐ Split ☐

[Here's a good question of obvious utility.] Have you ever contributed money to any political race? [That query will test the degree of commitment the responder has to the general political process.]
Yes (Contribute) ☐ No (Do not contribute) ☐

In summary, we now know if the person is knowledgeable, what percentage are knowledgeable and their degree of commitment to a particular issue and to the political process. Everybody has his own style, but usually structure the first two questions to be innocuous. This tends to put the respondent at ease, talking to the strange voice at the end of their phone.

The next question may be,

Do you intend to vote in the _____ election? or
How do you intend to vote on the _____ issue?

Keep in mind that polls are most valuable for the background they can provide. Before asking about anything else, it might be useful to ask: "What do you feel are the three or four most important issues facing residents of River City, like yourself?" Answers to this type of question allow respondents to set out their own issues.

Most novice pollsters will be amazed at how quickly trends develop and, in later polls, how quickly they change again. This is due in no small part to media influence. Media political commentators traditionally depreciate the issues that candidates in major races choose to articulate. As a practical matter, major politicians poll to find out the issues and then hit on these. When citizen issues are not similar to those chosen by professional commentators, the media will accuse the candidates of avoiding the issues.

"How can the problems you identify be resolved?" is another excellent question that will tell the group how effectively the issues are working. Or, in the case of candidates, one can ask who is best qualified to handle these issues, or a list of people can be read asking who of these can best handle the issues.

It may be helpful to determine the age and economic status of the responder. Do this with the question,

Your age can be characterized as 19–30 ☐   31–45 ☐
45 and above ☐

Sex, if needed, can be marked down by the interviewer, based on voice.

Some pollsters think one can determine economic status by asking about such things as auto ownership, home or boat ownership. We do not recommend this, as it involves too much guesswork. Ask directly about income if you want that information, softening the question by using broad income ranges.

Often it is appropriate to ask how long the respondent has lived in the community, especially if your state or community has stringent residency requirements.

At times it is helpful to place a somewhat obscure question in the conversation such as, "Do you believe that the mayor (governor) was fair and even-handed toward the _____ group during the last year?" This question can be phrased to use a bureaucrat's name or whatever is appropriate.

Rather than ask how the respondent plans to vote, one can ask: "Have you ever heard of the _____ (initiative, law, issue or candidate)?"

It may now be time to play hardball, asking,

As for the issues you feel are important to the (state, county, city), do you believe the (initiative, bond, law) will address these issues? Yes ☐   No ☐

One situation that becomes problematic (and hard on those at the phones) is created when the callers run into one number after another where the respondent has not registered, has not heard of the issue or does not care about the issue's resolution. However, the name recognition—or lack of it—for a candidate or for an issue tells the group quite a bit about how the issue is perceived in the community. These frustrations in seeking good results convey useful information, and therefore should be considered by the pollsters.

If those who know about the issue responded much differently from those who are uninformed, it may be necessary to generate additional publicity. If time is critical with an election or decision day approaching and there are no further opportunities for publicity, including paid media, it may be necessary ruthlessly to reorient the group's priorities.

Whatever questions are used, be diligent about testing them out on a fairly large sample group before going regionwide with the questions. Be certain that each question is simple, succinct and understood. Test to be sure that the words mean what the poll writers think they mean and that opportunity for proper input is offered. Questions that require more than simple qualifying statements by the interviewer are probably incorrectly worded. Often what seems like simple, straightforward queries prove to be confusing or defective. No poll should be done without an extensive trial run. Professional pollsters sometimes keep track of the people they have called. They then call the same people a few weeks later to see if some are changing their minds.

At times campaigns have been blessed with a super-abundance of limited-skill volunteer help. Polling is an ideal way to put these people to work. You can even use polling as a cross-check on your direct mail fund appeals, making the calls simultaneously with the mailings and comparing results.

Professional pollsters operate out of central coordinated phone banks. This is the best procedure but not an absolutely necessary one. Volunteers who have printed instructions plus a good supply of printed questionnaires can easily poll out of their homes. The trick is to brief the poll takers thoroughly and then keep in touch with them—if you can reach them by phone!

Compiling the data should be relatively straightforward. Even open-ended questions will quickly solidify into repetitive categories. Pollsters will find that they hear basically the same story over and over. Campaigners should, however, be alert to the first hints of subtle changes in responses.

Amateurs or first-time activists err seriously when they pass over or ignore analysis of the "undecided" voter. It is far more difficult to switch a "no" to a "yes" than an "undecided" to a "yes." Therefore, closely track the undecideds. When the noes outnumber the yeses, but the undecideds could still influence the outcome, there may be cause for hope. One's analysis should focus on the number of undecideds who have moved since the last poll was taken, where they have moved (Our Side or theirs), and where other undecideds have come from.

Once the data are compiled, campaign activists can look them over for clues as to how issues should be addressed, what is important, how effective the group public relations have been, how much they are getting for their money, and how people are likely to react at that moment. Some pollsters use scales of severity to indicate importance of issues to respondents.

When reviewing the data, keep the group's recent activities in mind so as to evaluate which devices are working and which are so-so. Be especially alert to shifts in issues. Shifts always occur. The important element is to be ahead of the power curve by knowing about these shifts as they develop, before the competition does. Polling must identify where the group can best spend its limited advertising dollars and energy, and when it should redefine and sharpen its strategies.

Other than calculated leaks for partisan political purposes, the results of one's polls should be held in the strictest confidence. This can be a problem when dealing with large numbers of volunteer workers. It is possible to secure reasonably good data related to the Other Side's polls by taking one of its volunteer callers to lunch.

Polls can be used by any group that seeks to change public opinion and to determine how it is doing at that task. Polls are a report card and wish list rolled into one. Even if no ultimate public vote is expected, they tell the group what is on people's minds and how citizens relate to the issues. We can know in advance if people support freedom or, on the other hand, fear the responsibility it brings.

Mock Polls

There are polls, and there are polls which look like polls but are really propaganda, aimed at sensitizing the population to an issue. For example, we once wished to have a road paved to save a client two hundred miles a day in freight costs between his two locations. But environmental groups were opposed and the road commissioners did not wish to antagonize them.

How did we solve this problem? By changing the whole focus of the issue from paving a road to saving children from possible harm from our trucks, even though no child had ever been injured.

We called every single phone number in a city through which my client's trucks passed and asked, "Do you object to the many X Company trucks that come through your city every day?" Suddenly, everyone in the city had a problem they'd not realized they had. Additional publicity in the local newspaper fanned the discontent. Soon, the people in the city were upset, they told the road commissioners as much, and we got our road.

Chapter 35

Credibility

Political Action Groups, like Rodney Dangerfield, frequently feel that "we don't get no respect." The complaint is voiced variously: "People won't listen to us or believe our information." Or, "Our opposition gets all the press with their outrageous, insupportable statements." Such comments all reflect a *lack of credibility,* perceived or real, and nothing except lack of money causes more grief for our Political Action Groups.

To a degree, it is a problem of our own making. Our groups often seem to want only tiny nibbles of the respect we could command if we acted as if we were entitled to it. Truth is, new groups tend to have as much credibility as they are willing to break off and run with; at least until they make some blunder. Agencies, the media and politicians are sensitive to a group's own perceived self-worth. They extend such respect as is implicitly demanded of them, but no more.

Our Side is continually amazed and dismayed by the clout that ragtag, poorly financed, poorly organized interventionist groups command. It can't all be attributed to media bias. We must look at our own situation from time to time, asking this hard question, "Would you buy programs from people such as ourselves?"

Questions of credibility become especially important when the group asks a key member or someone in the community to serve on the brain trust or board of directors, as group spokesman, or—most important—as the chairman of the finance committee. If we can't gain the respect of those sympathetic to our cause, we surely will get none from the enemy.

The following checklist is, for the most part, a summary of items already touched on in previous chapters. The ground should now be familiar, and these are precisely the items we look for when evaluating the credibility of a new group. The evaluation is, of course, subject to local conditions and to the regional perceptions of local citizens.

Dress for success. Articulate, well dressed, obviously well informed spokesmen are the first contact many people have with the group. A good first impression provides most of the initial— and then long-term—credibility. Dress is very important when building credibility, many times more so than what is initially said. This is not to say that group leaders should not be articulate and well informed, but to stress that they must dress for respect rather than look like clowns.

Numbers. The fact that the group represents a sizable number of voting citizens impresses the media and politicians as well as average citizens who are considering joining the group. One may not want to divulge the exact number of members initially. Just to maintain that "our large, obviously well-organized group is behind a given issue" adds credibility.

Organize seriously. Groups that have been organized for the long pull and that have been around for a while build respect for themselves. Doing a professional job in a detailed, thorough manner is part of the work that must be done to build credibility.

Permanence. Trappings of permanence foster credibility. Items such as furnished offices, telephone listings, letterhead stationery, business cards, office signs, etc., all lend credibility.

Set goals and stick to them. The existence of long-term plans and objectives adds credibility. Often this type of credibility occurs most in the mind of the group leaders, who then behave more credibly to those around them. In any event, the net effect is added credibility.

Publish—on schedule. Get your message out in a good quality format. Organization newsletters are credible, especially when the group succeeds in getting them out on a fairly regular schedule. Occasional, disorganized, badly-produced newsletters apologizing for being late have the opposite effect: they destroy group credibility.

If nothing works short of a lawsuit, sue. Past legal action generates present credibility. Both average citizens and the media realize the group is a player, serious about its goals, and willing to take action. In general it is not necessary for the group to win its suit to establish credibility.

Literature counts. Fact sheets and professionally planned brochures give the group respect.

Drop names if you can. Publishing a list of prominent supporters, especially if it is reasonably extensive, provides much credibility. Politicians often use this device shortly before election day.

Display your scalps. Having fought the bureaucracy to a standstill, either legally or in a public relations context, is an important element in credibility.

Cultivate media people. Be respectful and friendly with the media. A first-name basis with media people builds credibility. Someone in the group should know every media person on sight. This device is easily and inexpensively orchestrated.

The house list. Current, well organized, computerized lists of supporters and workers create credibility. The adage that twenty hard-core followers are more effective than a list of one thousand potentials, applies.

Laugh and the world laughs with you. A sense of humor helps immensely. Stiff, unbending, humorless, lemon-sucking groups are perceived as such and are treated like the collection of dolts they probably are.

Factoids. Unfortunately, in the current atmosphere the use of factoids seems not to discredit an organization. If they are used against your group, bend every effort at once to discredit the people who use them. If you can't stomach retaliating with factoids of your own, try some "factoids" that tell the truth.

Write letters. Extensive use of direct mail gives the public the impression that the group is well organized and powerful.

Raise and use money creatively. Thorough, attractive fund raising gives the group about as much credibility as having six figures in the bank. Using these funds is important. Unless the group is out in the marketplace creating some excitement with its funds, its credibility will wind down.

Poll! Polling gives the group an informational advantage that leads to credibility.

Speakers. Organizing and using a speakers bureau provide tremendous visibility along with the impression of organizational ability. These raise the credibility quotient, especially when the speakers are not the original organizers. This is a great way to get your message to the community.

Master the art of the press conference. Professionally done news conferences always raise a group's credibility. Average citizens don't usually believe that anyone would call a news conference unless he is credible.

Slide shows. Skillfully assembled and written slide shows make your message *interesting* and at the same time convey the impression that the group has really thought through the issues and is preparing for the long term.

Hang out a shingle. Professionally designed and painted signs on the door are very important. Initially many organizations "make do" with a piece of cardboard taped to the window. The sooner this temporary expedient is traded for a good-looking, permanent sign, the sooner the group will start benefiting from the credibility passers-by will ascribe to you because of your permanent-looking display.

Handle money correctly. Detailed, accurate budgets that complement the strategic plan provide credibility among one's members, especially financial supporters.

Testimony. If group representatives have testified before congressional or other legislative committees, it adds greatly to the group's stature. Publicize it.

Letters to the editor. Letters are neutral in and of themselves, but can add credibility with the newspaper if they are consistently well-informed, persuasive and grammatical. When there are other good reasons to send them, do so—knowing that the group's credibility will neither be particularly helped nor be hurt unless the letters are illiterate.

Coalitions. It isn't a certain credibility builder, but usually—depending on the circumstances—the group's credibility can be enhanced by entering into coalitions with other respected (or feared) Political Action Groups. At other times it may be politically expedient to cooperate with weaker groups, but keep public mention of these associations to a minimum. Each situation must be evaluated individually.

Winning is the whole point. Organizing to win is credible. Like World War II fighter pilots, we should go out to shoot the other guy down, not—as is too often the case—go out and serve as practice targets for the other side. Fight to win.

Show your strength. Listing one's complete membership roster over and above a selected list of heavy hitters can extend credibility, especially if the list is large. When some of the names are obscure, consider publishing the list with identifying titles. Don't publish if the group has made lots of noise but is relatively small.

Before running people's names in the paper, call everyone for permission to use his name. The authors have embarrassed opposition groups by locating people who hadn't wanted their names used in the paper as an endorsement, and were irate.

There are other items one can monitor that will tend to increase credibility. These, however, are the first ones we look for when doing a quick evaluation of the group's credibility potential. Fortunately, most of the above items are also part of a regular campaign, so should be familiar to users of this book.

Chapter 36

A Plan for Raising Money

M ore often than not, the first reason consultants are called onto the scene is to raise money. This is true because securing necessary funding is nearly always the biggest roadblock facing fledgling political activists. The ability to secure needed start-up funds is the original popularity "poll" that must be taken. In this business, there is no popular support without money and vice versa.

There are many effective methods of addressing the money raising question. The plan we first suggest is certainly not the only one that could be effective. However, from experience we know that it is one that will work. This plan will answer the question on everyone's mind—"How are we going to pay for all of this?"

The first necessity is to raise start-up money. This is the money needed to hire a consultant, open an office, commence regular fund raising activities, install phones, purchase letterhead, pay staff to develop a strategic plan, rent computers, start mailing lists and to do all of the many chores that absolutely must be done the first few days of a new campaign.

Start-up money can be raised using one of three common methods. Combinations will sometimes work, but usually take too long to implement. There is no time to spare when you're raising seed money. Stick to one of the three plans. They all start with the assumption that political actions are precipitated by a crisis, either real or imaginary. Whether or not there is a real crisis, and whatever happens, the participants must be galvanized into believing "We must do something—Now!"

In about 30 percent of the cases, the initial organizer will commit to the ultimate sacrifice by kicking in necessary funds from corporate or personal sources. It doesn't happen even half of the time, but probably all of us have known people who come to feel so strongly about a matter that securing a second mortgage on their homes and throwing the $30,000–$40,000 thus raised into the pot seems logical to them. Some hope to recover their investment after the project gets going but, in our experience, this is generally not a valid expectation. Don't count on getting your money back.

Other businessmen elect to mortgage or otherwise encumber their business, reasoning perhaps that the value of their business is materially diminished if the forces of the bureaucracy are allowed to dominate.

A more desirable situation results when eight or ten people decide to throw their money into a common pot. This is the most common method of raising start-up money, applying in perhaps 50 percent of the cases. These people will commit typically between one and three thousand dollars each, often in response to a leader/ organizer who says he is committing to the project. Asking these people to bring in two or three friends each is important. In this case, the initial impact spreads with a ripple effect, bringing in increasing numbers of supporters. There are, however, only a limited number of people who can and will come into any project in a given region or who even have the ability to contribute.

Businessmen, accustomed to making investments, are sympathetic to this approach. They know and understand the concept of using seed money. People who are employed as writers, teachers, mechanics, clerks and secretaries, for example, do not as readily accept this sort of "investment." Other techniques are employed to reach these people.

The downside to this device occurs when the original investors, quite naturally, decide that they must protect their investments by assuming the role of the project's governing board. One can say without reservation that these people cannot and should not become the brain trust. However, they could conceivably become a steering committee, assuming that they demonstrate they can reach decisions by consensus and can manage something of this magnitude.

A last start-up method is available to the inexperienced but motivated souls who have little background or ability to go to fat cats for seed money. These people must believe very strongly in the cause and be willing to get out on the street and work tirelessly at contacting people. These contacts are of the toughest type, done one at a time, whose small donations will be pooled together into a valid start-up fund.

It is best if this kind of organizer sells something in connection with the cause—newsletter subscriptions, a group membership, bumper stickers, political buttons, books, posters or T-shirts. Newsletters are usually best because they maintain contact with and the interest of the buyer. The other items are seldom more than devices to wring a few extra dollars out of interested people. Relatedly, all of us know about bake or garage sales as a fund raising device. These are fine and most people can manage them without too much trouble. Some hold block parties, art fairs, concerts; sell candy, cookies, flowers or whatever to raise money.

Professionals rarely get involved with these activities. Fund raising of this sort needs large amounts of volunteer labor and is so slow that it costs more to pay a political consultant to run a bake sale than is raised by that activity.

Little moneymakers work painfully slowly—an inch at a time at the most optimistic level. Sheer guts and persistence alone carry the day. On the plus side, the device is available to almost anyone, regardless of political experience.

The big drawback with "little money" projects shows up later in crossing from a pure amateur effort to the next, professional phase of the project. It takes vision and guts to turn over funds scraped together a dollar at a time to a $4,000 per month (if he's inexpensive and committed) professional who then carries on with the project.

The authors cannot cite a single example of a freedom-oriented organization starting its life in this manner. Dozens of proregulatory lobbies have started in this manner but Our Side seldom, if ever, proceeds in this fashion. Perhaps it is the curse of the self-employed or business-owning class to have so little time that work must produce results or the work must be abandoned.

Sustaining Fund Raising

Having raised the needed start-up money, the group now has several options available. Wise organizers quickly resort to many, if not all, of them.

With money in hand for offices, phone, staff and stationery, one can—in good conscience and with realistic expectations—go to a heavy-hitter and ask him to chair the group's fund raising efforts. Although it need not always be so, generally the more "combative" male will more often be likely to put the bite effectively on his peers for money. We do not know why things work this way and wish it were otherwise, but this has been our experience.

We try to give rules to cover most fund raising situations. The rule for choosing a fund raising committee chair is simple: *Successful chairmen of fund raising committees must be senior members of the moneyed community in which they operate!*

Or put another way: Rich people know rich people; rich people trust other rich people; rich people don't usually give money to other people at all, but on the rare occasions they do, it is almost invariably to another rich person.

This fellow must have enough stature among the targeted support groups so that when he places a call to his peers, secretaries recognize his name and put the call through. The man must also be of sufficient reputation so that the callee will go ahead and take the call.

Publicly acknowledging the fact that the chairman has donated, say, $20,000 of his own funds to the campaign goal of $160,000 will do wonders when the fund raising chairman calls the lesser lights. Of course, the chairman must be a person with the ability to take this kind of action. People who are solicited by this type of person usually are not afraid to be financially co-identified with his winning cause.

Finding a heavy hitter chairman for the group's fund raising efforts is always difficult but not impossible if one observes a few simple facts of heavy hitter life:

- Heavy hitters always want to be reasonably certain that the cause is going to succeed. They are not accustomed to political speculation. Before getting involved, they will require a thorough professional briefing, involving all of the issues both pro and con.

- Heavy hitters are reassured by staffers whom they perceive to be professional. A potential heavy hitter who looks out and sees good management and technical people on the project as well as able shirtsleeve board members will have a markedly higher confidence level.
- Take care of the picky details of a campaign. Heavy hitters will expect someone else to handle them and do not want to become enmeshed with micromanagement.
- Knowing that the board has already raised some funds and that the project is financially viable in the intermediate sense will impress potential fund raising chairmen of the type the group requires.
- Be careful of the motives one plays on when talking to potential fund raising chairmen. Usually it is best to assume they have seen it all. As a rule, it is tough to impress them by invoking their Patriotic Duty or the Good of the Community. They are always impressed far more with the first three elements listed than with philosophical arguments.

The board should anticipate that the chairman of the fund raiser will very likely want to include several friends on his fund raising committee. It is not uncommon for a suitable person to defer making a decision regarding the project till he has talked with his immediate circle of friends. If they agree that it is a winnable issue and offer to help, the fellow will usually move ahead.

Staff support for a high-powered chairman must be superb. A super efficient secretary—either the group's or the man's own business secretary—must always be there to handle letters, take calls and generally accomplish the detail work these people expect. Bookkeeping people must be alerted to the possible need to provide additional information for the finance committee. Often they ask for a daily accounting of the money that came in and was paid out. The committee may require extensive computerized lists of names, tied to the date they were contacted, with the date they contributed and the actual deposit of their checks interfaced against the master list of potential donors.

One of the first tasks of the finance chair will be to develop a list of potential donors. This list will be assembled in part by the board, the fund raising committee, the fund chairman, the brain trust, the campaign manager and any others who agree to help. The list should include names of businesses and individuals, contacts in business, addresses, phone numbers, and—most important of all—an estimate of how much the chairman believes he can squeeze out of each person. Don't forget about similar organizations, PACs, sugar daddies, etc., as you search for principled subscribers.

When developing this list of heavy hitters, it will take the staff a minimum of three times longer than it first supposed to look up all the names and to verify the telephone numbers and addresses. It is a disaster to list a number on the heavy hitter call sheet only to have the fund chairman call and find out it is an incorrect number. The group will have a good indication that it has the correct fund chairman when he gets out his own address book to note down the unlisted numbers of many of the people on the list.

Putting down a targeted amount of money on the donors' list for which to ask is extremely tricky. As a general rule a person's status is either diminished or enhanced by the amount of money requested. Ask too little and you're insulting. Ask too much and he is flattered but will not write the check. The correct amount will both flatter and result in a check being written.

Activities of the fund raising group are best kicked off with a news conference and a notice in the newsletter. Other efforts to sign up new members and to accumulate additional signatures should continue unabated. New people add to the perceived groundswell of the project, pay for the phone and lights, and provide a pool of volunteers to handle the many tasks the group faces.

Squeezing the fat cats is important, but one should not neglect the skinny cats. Solicitation letters should be prepared for mailing to the lists that have been developed or that were purchased. Direct mail fund solicitation is expensive but can be cost-effective nevertheless. Use funds generated by the fund raising committee to do the first mailings.

Follow the guidelines in chapter 21 for designing a fund appeal letter. Pick the best, most suitable elements from several, combining them into one return mailer that suits the group's needs. Commercial printers always have many examples from which to work, if all else fails. The authors' personal choice is to put a picture of whatever it is we are trying to work on—such as a school, an airport, or even a bureaucrat's office—on the flap. This is where placing a picture of the school we intend to build—or which was closed by the bureaucrats—the factory we wish to attract or protect, the picture of the small businessmen who are unable to continue or any other appropriate pictorial message is very valuable as a means of selling something specific. Then put in an ample number of blank lines and ask for comments. People may leave them blank but sometimes it is amazing what they will tell the group.

It works best to have specific items to sell and check off on the envelopes. Start small with items such as one tank of gas for the car—$20 worth—on up to the office rent at $400, the next direct mailing at $3,500 or the October opinion survey at $6,500. All of these seem to attract additional funds from people who are more inclined to donate if they know exactly how their money will be spent.

Some proregulation groups have successfully gone to the taxpayers for assistance. As a general rule, this device does not impress most freedom-oriented political activists. We prefer to sell our wares in the most persuasive manner possible, in the open marketplace, leaving grants and government loans alone.

As soon as funds are available, the group should undertake solicitation of funds in regional papers and magazines. As a general rule, professionally drawn ads asking for support are just about a wash. Expect them to bring in about as much as they cost to draw up and run in the paper. The problem is that they are very pricey on the front end to get into the paper. Their advantage on the back end, assuming they do break even financially, is that they get the word out to large numbers of people at no net cost to the group. They also provide additional names for the computer list.

There are several additional tactics that customarily make up the plan of action for an effective fund raising effort.

Expand the list of potential heavy hitters that the fund chairman can personally contact. To an extent this will occur in the normal course of events. Nevertheless, it may be wise to sit down again with the board members ten weeks into the project, asking them who additionally can be placed on the fund chairman's list. As a practical matter, this may be an ongoing staff function. It will always be incumbent on the staff to keep an accurate record of who has been contacted, who is dragging his feet, who said absolutely no and who should be asked again by somebody different.

As mentioned, when new skinny cats are added to the list, they should be sent fund raising letters asking for a donation. Those who do not respond should be tagged in the computer. The group may elect to send other letters with a slightly different approach. These may be more effective, especially at times when the group is generating extensive publicity in the media and via the newsletter. Bulk mass mail solicitations should be planned to run on a predetermined schedule along with their supporting activity.

All of this is easy to summarize on paper. Like writing one million dollars, one can more easily describe dollar figures than earn them. As with everything else in politics, there are many pitfalls in the field of fund raising. Other tactics should always be under consideration.

Squeezing the faithful under emergency conditions is an excellent example worth describing in depth to illustrate the point. Novice and veteran alike will groan at the complexity and perhaps even the ethics of this device. Remember, when one's back is against the wall, options narrow dramatically. Devices that once were considered borderline look more and more acceptable.

Telemarketing is one technique which was once considered borderline but has now been developed to a science. Although the dreaded call at dinner hour alienates a certain percentage of possible contributors, the system works. If it didn't work, big companies wouldn't be phoning you at dinner.

Telemarketing's big advantage is almost cash. The grist for the phone mill is the same list used for direct mail. Telemarketing is easier than direct mail, because it can be organized for any evening in any empty office with a multiline phone system. If the group has enough money, the group office should be equipped beforehand with five or ten phones. The phone bank will pay for itself many times over in a single campaign, and can be used or rented out for other purposes between periods of peak need.

You can use the phone bank to organize demonstrations, find seed funding, fill a special-purpose coffer or even phone the faithful on the day after the election to inform them that the group needs so many dollars to retire debt. Particularly effective is calling previous donors you haven't heard from for a while.

Phone banks are useful for double-dipping an existing mailing list. Generally people who respond to phone solicitation won't respond to mail, and the reverse is also true. So, you may double the effective pull of a single list by working it once by mail, and once by phone.

A phone campaign will also give you one important view you don't get from mail. People who don't respond to mail are invisible to your group. They don't say why they don't respond. A quick call on the phone may tell you why.

During the last week of the campaign when the media are full of items regarding the project and everyone knows decision day looms, run a current computer printout listing everyone's name, address and phone number and the amount and date of his contribution. This assumes that during hectic times this information is kept current ... not always a valid assumption. Using this master list, again contact everyone by phone who has contributed, making a last-minute impassioned plea for additional funds with which to put the project over the top.

Obviously this is a last-ditch measure, best used if there really is an emergency. Reportedly it was conceived and first tested by Democrat presidential hopefuls who found that they netted from 20 to 30 percent of the funds they got on the first round. At a time when an additional $10,000 for TV spots or legal fees, for instance, might put the project over the top, such a measure may be well worth the effort.

The finance chairman or members of his committee should make these calls. They are time-consuming and difficult to handle successfully. Normally, few people will agree to take on this sort of work.

Corporate and private donors customarily ask about the tax status of their gifts to Political Action Groups. In an estimated 80 percent of the cases, fast-moving Political Action Groups do not have time to file for tax-exempt status. Although it would undoubtedly be extended, many groups are organized only for relatively short terms and would be out of existence by the time a ruling came down. It is best, under the circumstances, either to sell donors something they can deduct if they must have a tax deduction or, more simply, to tell supporters there is no time to seek tax-exempt status.

This constitutes the general plan of attack for fund raising. As mentioned, it is the most commonly requested information from political consultants. This chapter—in and of itself—should accomplish our objective of providing a specific item that is easily worth the price of the book.

Chapter 37

Potpourri

Here we discuss, in no particular order, relatively minor campaign tactics that do not warrant lengthier treatment.

Truth Squad

When engaged in a rough, no-holds-barred campaign, and when the issues are complex and easily muddied by the opposition, consider setting up a truth squad. Its responsibility would be to clarify the issues and keep the public focused. It would call attention to every false claim and every attempt to duck or obscure issues by the Other Side.

The squad should be staffed with quick-witted people who know the subject thoroughly. Their ability as public speakers should be the best the group can turn out. Squad members must have all of the data and facts on the contested subject at their fingertips, along with references to experts that substantiate their positions. In the past, truth squads used weighty, indexed reference books. With the advent of portable computers with access to large databases on disk or using modems, the books are mostly gone and truth squads have a better weapon—a laptop computer.

Members of the squad should attend every public meeting, news conference and citizen rally held by the opposition. Initially it takes a bit of sleuthing by the campaign staff to determine when and where the opposition plans to meet. However, after only a few appearances, the media will usually call campaign headquarters with this information, hoping for a more controversial story.

198

Truth squad members should wear name tags identifying themselves. Their job is to note down the inconsistencies, errors, incorrect data, erroneous conclusions and any other dubious remark by opposition speakers. They usually tape record the meeting to get a permanent record.

If, after the meeting, the squad can point out even one factual error or a place where the truth was stretched, it will tend to destroy the other side's credibility, especially if the issues are complex. The existence of a truth squad will draw media like frogs to bugs. If your people are at the meeting and the media know who they are, they will invariably be asked to comment.

At times the truth squad will actually generate more coverage than the opposition at its own news conference. However, media people usually support the regulatory side of most issues, so be glad for anything you can get. Your truth squad will improve its results by honing its skills, cultivating the media, and learning how to say just enough to get the kill. The media don't want to listen to interminable arguments, so be quick and deadly.

The announcement that a truth squad has been formed is itself often good for some excellent publicity. The implication, of course, is that the squad had to be formed because the Other Side is playing loose with the truth or acting disreputably. Play that up at the initial press conference, without overdoing it.

At this time, the group spokesman should tell news conference attendees: "We are dealing with a complex, technical issue that is easily distorted in ways the public may not understand. We see a tendency for those involved to play fast and loose with the facts. Evidently, they think they can put one over on the public. We're here to tell them that they can't. We have put together an excellent group of research analysts who will examine all the data and every claim that the powers-that-be make. Then they will tell you what the facts really are. They will document every figure, every fact and every number they give you. Members of the truth squad will make every effort to be out where citizens can ask questions and receive solid, clear, documented answers."

Finding courageous people who will go into the lion's den, identify themselves and withstand the abuse from the opposition is often a problem. When done properly, these courageous people can turn hostility into a public relations bonanza, especially when dealing with the bureaucracy.

Truth squads function best when the group has several intelligent, studious-sounding people who can be supported by volunteer or paid staff able to undertake large amounts of meticulous research. As a general rule, this research is handled by long-suffering, hard-working, motivated volunteers. Unless all these people are available, along with several articulate committee members, the group should pass this device by.

Truth squads that have not done their homework are easily discredited. Answers and documentation can be delivered in a slightly amateurish, bumbling fashion but let the truth squad issue one insupportable statement or (God forbid) one untruth and the whole effort will blow up in the group's face.

Setting up telephone hot lines manned by trained volunteer staffers is becoming popular as a type of less threatening, less rigorous form of truth squad.

During a recent battle over landfill legislation, the group set up a hot line number where people could call to receive a recorded message. Before the message started we asked callers to give their names, addresses and phone numbers. This discouraged some crank calls. At the end of the message callers were encouraged to stay on the line if they had additional questions on the issue. About 60 percent were satisfied with the recorded message and hung up. All callers were subsequently sent a brochure and eventually a request for funds. Collections from this group were minimal but did pay for the mailings.

Rumor Mongering

We have never felt it was necessary, effective or appropriate to use rumors in a campaign. But beware, this is a device used against our friends time after time. Once, as our team looked more and more successful in a campaign, we found that the opposition increasingly resorted to a program of professionally coordinated, well-planned rumor mongering.

Our "real" reasons for favoring a freedom issue were often questioned in the wildest terms. Such items as a board member's marital fidelity and our financial honesty, along with our "ulterior" motives, were questioned in most unreasonable contexts. Often the friends of regulations feel it is crucial to make a huge issue out of the fact that we might profit from a certain course of events. Perhaps this is the greatest insult they feel they can hurl. Most people who earn their own bread without benefit of government don't understand this insult, however.

The rule is to get everyone out on the street when rumors surface. Counter such rumor mills by placing your supporters out and about where everyday citizens can have ample opportunity to ask any questions they feel appropriate. If you as a group have been doing your job in an honest, timely fashion in the newsletter and with the slide show and fact sheet, you have little to fear. Rumors generally do not relate to actual complex campaign issues. Allowing the amateur membership to handle them is not risky.

Freedom issues seem especially conducive to rumor. Recently we helped a group seeking the freedom to start small businesses. It was accused by rumor of wanting the freedom to bring gambling and prostitution into the state. We put some sweet, elderly ladies out on the firing line and they made the charges look so ludicrous that we actually had a favorable backlash.

Parliamentary Procedure

It is a fact of life that whoever knows the group's rules best can control that group most effectively. The supplemental rule is that one should belong to as many different groups (on both sides) as possible. In some cases one can influence the groups, in others there is much to be learned about their plans and tactics, just sitting and listening or reading the newsletter. Membership in many groups can give the impression of more strength than actually exists. But more about this concept later in this chapter.

At times it is appropriate purposely to tie a group into knots using parliamentary procedures so as to preclude it from taking effective action.

It is possible to act the pious peacemaker, suggesting that a heated proposal be tabled until an unspecified time in the future. Under one group's rules it took a simple majority to table the measure but a two-thirds majority to lift it from the table. Under those circumstances the motion to table effectively killed the proposal, because there were never enough votes to overturn it.

In another zoning fight, there was a colluding, fearless player who would second every motion, no matter how ridiculous. We attached amendment after amendment to routine motions, which required the full board to take up measures ranging from cutting the commission's funding to zero to doing away with all application requirements.

A friend on a school board made use of continual motions to adjourn, which is a nondebatable, time-consuming motion. At times he successfully cut the meetings off before essential staff action could be approved. It worked only occasionally, and that mostly because he was a master at parliamentary procedure. But when it did, the entire bureaucracy ground to a halt. When the bureaucracy tried to do routine housekeeping chores without board approval, he successfully accused it of impropriety.

This ploy usually requires two bold, knowledgeable people who study group rules in detail. It is not often useful but it can provide a toehold in an otherwise impossible situation.

Multiple-Group Ploy

While working on agricultural issues in California, author Larry Grupp discovered that a gaggle of environmentalist antipesticide groups which were giving the farmers a tough time had virtually the same boards of directors. In other words, a group opposing pesticides was formed and generated a membership; then most of the same board set up a second and even a third group, all addressing the same issue. Organizers of all the groups were the same people.

When appealing for public support and going to the media, one group could support another and vice versa. The multiple effect this device provided was devastating. At hearings these people testified at soporific length supporting each other's factoids and recommending more and more irrational action. At times, members of the groups registered as individuals, giving yet more and more adverse testimony, till the bureaucrats could not help believing they were faced with an absolute groundswell.

Having had to counter it, we can give a hearty recommendation as to the effectiveness of cloning PAGs. There is no reason Our Side cannot do the same.

Self-Funding Newspaper and TV Ads

This tactic is already well-known in the trade but is often not seriously considered. It is often not used because campaign headquarters fear that they will lose control of their media scheduling. Nevertheless, this device constitutes a very effective type of fund raising that takes advantage of a donor's disposition to know exactly what his money is buying.

The tactic works as follows. Central campaign staff people oversee the production of professional ad copy. In the case of radio, they produce and duplicate messages on cassettes. For TV they produce and duplicate video cassettes of the group's commercials. All ads are finished, ready for actual use. Newspaper copy is produced camera-ready.

Campaign staffers call local supporters, asking them if they will run one or more of the group's commercials on TV, radio or in the newspaper, as appropriate. These same staffers will already know how much the ad will cost to run locally and the time slots still available. The staffer will explain to the local supporter that the central association wants badly to use the commercial but that no funds remain. Often the supporter will agree to send a limited amount of money along as a "best effort" contribution to get things moving.

It will then be incumbent on the local group to go out and beat the bushes for additional funds. Usually the existence of the copy that it can demonstrate and the booking deadline will provide enough incentive to get local supporters talking to their friends. As a working device it will either draw the local group members together, giving them a goal, or prove to be their undoing as a result of the impossibility of the situation in which they find themselves.

Possibilities exist that local supporters will scale down the ad or run it fewer times, making it less effective, or they may miss deadlines, possibly throwing the media campaign into disarray. Political activists must evaluate their local situations to decide if these possibilities would pose problems.

Waiver of Rules

An associate was once told by an unusually arrogant bureaucrat that her request was impossible since it clearly violated the rules under which that bureaucrat worked. The incident had to do with issuing a map showing proposed school district boundaries.

The lady was so incensed by the incident that she developed a very formal-looking printed document titled "Request for Waiver of Rules." She provided blanks for listing the bureaucrat's full name, title and grade, and full name of the office, the congressional authorization for the office, the person's immediate supervisor and an exact citation of the rule that precluded the bureaucrat from acting. At the end of the document, done in the most serious, straightforward, professional fashion, she placed spaces to list reasons why the rules should be waived, who could waive them, and a formal, notarized, signed statement asking that they be waived.

The lady has used or threatened to use the sheet dozens of times. Always, she says, the fear of a form that looks so official and authoritative gives bureaucrats the willies. It nearly always jars them out of their beloved "procedures."

"In a face to face confrontation, they virtually always grant me the information I request," she maintains, "no matter what rules and regulations may originally be cited."

Community Action Columns of the Local Paper

Now and then small groups, addressing a minor matter and having limited time and resources, can seek relief by sending a letter to the local newspaper's Community Action column. The tactic works especially well when someone has been severely dealt with on a relatively insignificant matter.

These letters should very clearly and thoroughly set out the problem while being the model of brevity. At times these letters will even alert the papers to a possible story idea. At worst, they provide a bit of publicity for the issue even if the matter remains unresolved.

Campaign Photographer

At the time the group puts its slide show together it will discover that a sharp amateur or semiprofessional photographer is an inestimable asset.

Photos of a bureaucrat closing a business, impounding a vehicle or confiscating the tools of a person's trade are one-time events that, if captured on film, are invaluable. The only better situation is the deployment of a video camera by the group. Cameras can be a cheaper substitute for a video camera and, in most circumstances, average citizens have a better concept of how to use them. In any event, a camera is more likely to be handy.

When the issues of the campaign involve possible police action by the bureaucracy, a camera is a defensive weapon. Purchase a number of cheap cameras, load them with fast film and fresh batteries and distribute them to people likely to suffer actual physical abuse.

Advertisements in the papers often require photos. Hiring a photographer can be expensive and may not produce the same results as a patient, dedicated volunteer. It isn't a top priority, but make it a practice to try to recruit a photographer for work during a campaign. The person may also know how to operate the video equipment, and that's another big plus.

Rating Legislators and Bureaucrats

This is an effective tactic that generates easy publicity.

A little group—only seven people!—organized to try to force the state to pass laws that would limit the counties' ability to raise property taxes. We had little clout and less money. But we did have some savvy people in the group.

Media attention to our cause was minimal. Legislators did not pay us much heed. Then one of our members hit on the idea of doing a Legislator's Spending Rating.

We titled the project "Who Speaks for the Taxpayer?"

Collectively, we analyzed all of the spending bills in the recently concluded session of the state legislature to determine who voted for and who voted against spending any money. Dollar amounts in the spending bills were represented as points. If a legislator voted "yes" to spend a thousand dollars he got a thousand points. A "no" vote earned him a thousand negative points. There were about thirty-five spending bills in that little state that year.

The legislators who ended up with the fewest points were assigned a percentage value as measured against a theoretical limit of voting "no" every time. Admittedly the system was not entirely fair, but it did tag the big spenders in the state.

Anybody with a rating of over 65 percent was listed as a Frugal Friend of the Taxpayer. We even got letters out on our stationery, from our minuscule group, commending those with high ratings for their public-minded thriftiness. Those in the 45 to 65 percent bracket were labeled Friends, those in the 20 to 44 percent range were labeled Big Spenders. Legislators receiving 19 percent or less were labeled Reckless Big Spenders.

The day we got our letters of commendation out to the top twelve or fourteen out of eighty-five legislators, we called a news conference. One of the members made a chart listing every legislator by name and showing how he stood in the rating.

Every paper in the state covered the rating. We made every TV station. For two days our phone rang off the hook with calls from reporters who wanted to know about how we did the rating and how their local people did, exactly.

A number of irate legislators also called. Obviously we had hit them where it hurt.

The device is easy to implement. The secretary of state has everyone's voting record or can tell you where to get it. Pick out between five and thirty-five key bills having to do with the group's cause, check them for "yes" or "no" votes and then correlate them against a 100 percent standard. It is a bit tricky thinking up a catchy title to hang on the bad guys at the news conference, but we proved that even as few as seven can think up something effective.

Ratings are done by many larger national groups but rarely in local circumstances. We recommend this device in state and local situations. It is guaranteed to garner publicity and credibility for even tiny groups.

The tactics we've discussed here show that creativity can help level the playing field for everyone who is determined to regain freedom usurped by the common bureaucratic enemy.

Chapter 38

The Future: The Truth Shall Make You Free

Political activism is much like warfare. One deploys his forces, using the best intelligence and whatever resources are available, in the most efficient manner possible, to hit the enemy where he is weakest. Politics is also like warfare in that the side that most effectively deploys the latest technology usually wins the contest. Today, the most potent weapon in politics is the computer. For freedom fighters, it is an instrument of truth.

Look at one example of computer power. From 1984 to 1988 the Republican National Committee is accurately reported to have spent close to $5 million creating computerized data banks for use in the campaign for president. Some of this information was superfluously collected on Gary Hart, Paul Simon and people like John Glenn. But, as the *Wall Street Journal* reported, George Bush was always light years ahead of any possible Democrat candidate regarding possession of information on file. Michael Dukakis, as a result, found himself unable to take the high ground during the campaign. He continually reacted to Bush. Never, during the entire campaign, was he able to capture any semblance of an initiative.

Time after time the Republicans proved that they knew every public utterance made by Dukakis as unearthed and catalogued by their Presidential Opposition Research Group. Nothing is more embarrassing to the opposing politician than quoting him taking the other side of an issue in the past, making unfulfilled promises, waffling, or making blunders. They were ready every time Dukakis spoke out on any issue in any place. They proved that high-tech candidates will, in the future, control huge research operations that will provide more information about their opponents than the victims can remember about themselves. Even on the local level and in initiative campaigns, political contests are going to be won and lost in the library. Computers and the wealth of information they make instantly available are providing the decisive edge. Battling the bureaucracy, fighting bond initiatives, duking it out with EPA people, or even running for a local school board seat, will all be done electronically, and done better.

Researchers able to enter data in an orderly, quickly retrievable manner in laptop computers are already replacing small armies of researchers and secretaries in local campaigns. Using little more than a desktop computer, a determined, persevering activist can research issues in depth. When the time is right, a group of only a few can unleash more havoc on tyrants than was ever considered possible, even with a far larger group of articulate activists.

In one case we asked our computer whizzes to program our computers to produce walking lists of neighborhoods in a medium-sized city in which we were battling out an initiative election. These lists were developed from city directories and from city utility department listings. The printouts contained everyone known to be living at a given address. The computer also determined the most efficient route to use to canvass the city.

Using their walking lists, our volunteers blitzed the city a neighborhood at a time. Our volunteers strode confidently up to the door knowing exactly who lived there, if they voted in any of the last three elections and how they registered (Democrat or Republican) in the last primary. At each house the volunteer circled the name of the person to whom he talked, and circled a code indicating how the occupant felt about our issue and another code indicating which of six stock letters to send to that address. That night campaigners fed the lists back into the computer, entering the codes.

Next morning the appropriate, previously prepared letters were sent, urging the recipient—addressed by name—to:

1. Continue supporting the effort by voting no.
2. Please reconsider your decision not to vote.

3. Reconsider voting against us for reasons of lower taxes.
4. Reconsider voting against us for the good of your children.
5. Reconsider voting against us for the good of city and county.
6. Reconsider voting against us because of your neighbors who have already decided to vote no.

Most had their personalized letters in their mail boxes the next day. Our volunteers didn't even have to be particularly bold or articulate using this system. Our letters handled the issue in a manner in which the polls suggested would be effective.

During the 1992 presidential campaign, Bill Clinton deployed thousands of paid and volunteer workers around the country. Each had a computer connected by modem to central campaign headquarters in a sort of electronic hub, spokes and wheel system.

Clinton used this extensive electronic mail system to send messages to local leaders, activists and surrogate spokesmen. When rival Bush traveled to Denver, for instance, local campaign headquarters got a complete advance text of his remarks along with a list of pertinent questions developed by the opposition research team. These questions were planted on area reporters by local workers.

All of the answers Bush gave in response were carefully recorded by Clinton supporters who immediately checked into the nearest office with a phone where they transcribed the answers plus the basic text as delivered and sent them back to headquarters verbatim. In Miami, that same night, Clinton used the remarks made by Bush at noon to blast him out of the water. Next morning Bush found he started the day just a little bit further behind.

Every day every Clinton laptop computer was sent complete information as to what had happened as few as eight hours ago. This current information flow tended to keep everyone's interest high. Supporters were getting information that was so current it was considered virtually "insider" in nature. Along with this information, headquarters sent the current topic of the day to every city surrogate. His duty was to soften up the voters by floating upcoming issues and policies. Always, everyone spoke with one voice, even on complex issues. This is virtually impossible without computer links.

Computers allow campaign managers to win the battle against their two most pervasive dragons, time and detail. Scheduling, which is always trouble—especially for small, local campaigns—can be handled by only one person. For instance, the computer may already be programmed to know how long it takes to drive from Danville to Springfield or from Moab to Vernal; or it can check if flights are available, when they depart and arrive, and their cost; what motels are available; and every other scheduling detail.

Computers generate personalized fund raising letters, that is, tailored to the recipients' wants, needs and propensity to respond. In this and every other circumstance, they can be used to determine the most effective use of the group's time and money. If money forces a choice between doing another mailing and a third poll, properly programmed campaign computers can demonstrate which options are better.

Records containing names of volunteers, duties they are interested in assuming, addresses and phone numbers, will be relatively easy to maintain. When volunteer time is limited, computers containing previous voting patterns can keep one's workers out of the precincts where residents are unlikely to vote. Media buys can be made by district in places where polls show the greatest likelihood of a shift in opinion.

Many otherwise time-consuming and dull campaign activities such as fund raising, voter registration, literature search, canvassing, media placement and coordination will be carried out by fewer people making fewer mistakes. People in this business often observe that the side that makes the fewer mistakes, wins. Computers provide that happy circumstance.

Political activists of the future who demonstrate the ability to harness the awesome capacities of their computers will gain inexorably in power. There may even be some leveling of the playing field as amateurs who know relatively little about politics but much about computers take on the entrenched bureaucracy. The right person in the right place at the right time could conceivably single-handedly recover huge amounts of freedom.

Computers cause old-fashioned low-tech political activists to make mistakes. They keep accurate track of what a bureaucrat can and cannot do. Partisan candidates find that by their second stop in a day their strategy must be completely revamped. At a morning coffee for supporters, for instance, the candidate may find that all that is accomplished is to respond to an opponent's charges. By lunch the hapless candidate is doing little but trying to stamp out additional brush fires set by the opposition.

We must seize every opportunity to learn all about computers, and use them to advantage in future campaigns. Of all methods and devices, computer research and database access seem to hold the greatest promise for lovers of freedom.

Afterword

We reflexively agree that without government intervention in the home and the work place, every citizen would be far better off. We even agree that this freedom must include the liberty to fail ignominiously if this is what our actions warrant. But we too often forget the human material we work with and for.

The human factor more than all the political rules determines whether we will succeed or fail. People who plan political actions must spend the time and devote their best thought to getting all of the human, social factors involved just right. In that regard, we may have done some readers of this book a disservice. Perhaps we made everything look as though it could be done by the numbers when really this is not quite true.

If the process doesn't come to terms with the human creature as he is, it won't work with people. Intuition and sympathy are as important as intelligence. Inspiration and uplift attract better than potential political gain and count more than political cost. The *impression*—not the fact—of humanitarianism has carried the interventionist agenda into our homes and businesses. We must be the more humanitarian in *fact* to restore the liberty and moral values we have lost.

Those of us who want government out of our daily lives are sometimes so dedicated to principle that we forget the human element. That will defeat us.

The Other Side makes a great many errors as well. We know that the team that makes the fewer errors usually wins the contest.

We can afford to make some errors but we can't afford to sit on the sidelines. We have so seldom even been in the game in recent decades, we may even enjoy an element of surprise. In any case we must see to it that we make fewer mistakes than players in the bureaucracy and in interventionist coalitions.

Conditions change constantly, and that is all the opportunity we need. Now we have to frame our enduring principles in new human terms to bring out the best in ourselves and in everyone we ask to follow us. We know we stand for the right. Let this be the central message not only in what we say but also in the way we seek to put things right in the political arena.

Good luck to all.